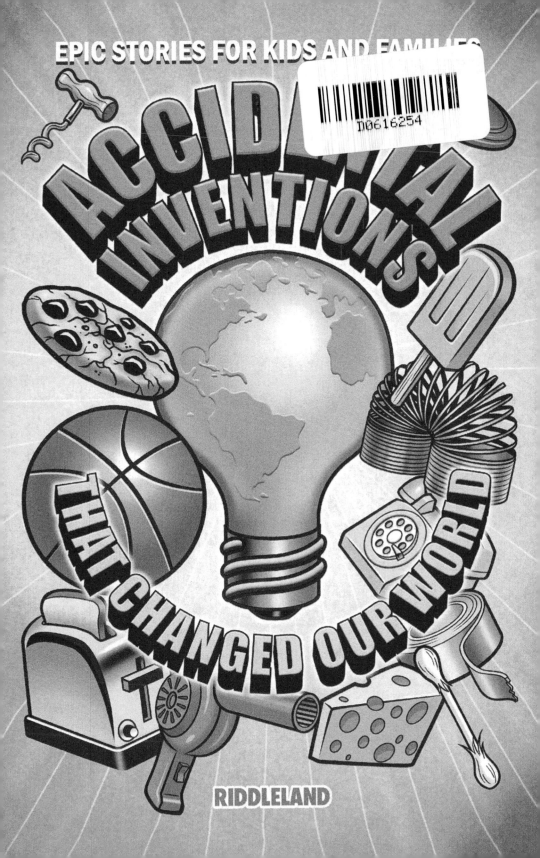

EPIC STORIES FOR KIDS AND FAMILIES

ACCIDENTAL INVENTIONS

THAT CHANGED OUR WORLD

RIDDLELAND

Table of Contents

Chapter Two: Accidental Invention of Toys

Chapter Three: Accidental Invention of Medicines and Medical Devices

Chapter Four: Technology and Electronics

Chapter Five: Accidental Inventions in the Kitchen

Chapter 6: Accidental Inventions Around the House 113

Riddleland Bonus

Join our Facebook Group at
Riddleland For Kids to get daily jokes and
riddles.

Bonus Book

FUN RIDDLES
AND
silly jokes
—— FOR ——
KIDS AND FAMILY

50 bonus
riddles, jokes and funny stories

RIDDLELAND

SCAN ME

https://pixelfy.me/riddlelandbonus

Thank you for buying this book. As a token of our appreciation,
we would like to offer a special bonus—a collection of 50
original jokes, riddles, and funny stories.

Introduction

"There are no rules. That is how art is born, how breakthroughs happen. Go against the rules or ignore the rules. That is what invention is about."
~ Helen Frankenthaler

Some inventions come about because someone noticed a problem and set about to resolve that problem. The inventor could envision a solution, and he or she sought to create what was seen. The inventor spent hours at the drawing board and in the lab, creating models and testing them. Failure often followed failure until one day - aha! Success! For instance, it took Thomas Edison over 100 times of not inventing the lightbulb to successfully build one.

The inventions in this book, though, were not envisioned by the inventor. These inventions 'just happened'; the inventor was not trying to create them. Some of them, such as gunpowder, were mistakes made while trying to invent something else. Some, such as the gas pump, began as something else, but the inventor saw a new use for the existing product. Others, meanwhile, resulted from happenchance, such as the popsicle.

In all cases, the inventors had to realize what they had. On the surface, what they had looked like trash, and many of those around them likely urged them to get rid of it. In fact, some inventions such as Super Glue were discarded when originally created and were rediscovered by someone else. However, in all cases the inventor saw potential in the invention. The inventor realized that what didn't work in one area, might work well in another.

Do you realize what you are about to read? These are not just stories of accidental inventions; they are stories of inspiration. They are a reminder to look for the good in ourselves and in others. They are also a reminder to keep our eyes open; life is full of opportunities. In fact, what often looks like a failure can be the beginning of something great.

Here are the stories of 60 common everyday items that were invented by accident. You will be amazed at how some things came to be. (Although all the stories have been researched, different people remember things slightly differently, and so some details may or may not be what happened.) Once you have finished the adventures, we will talk again at the conclusion of the book. The stories can be read in any order; I personally like to go from 1 to 60, but I know some people like to skip around. If you enjoy a particular adventure, each story has references so you can learn more about that invention. You will have heard - and likely used - most of these inventions. Of course, a couple of these inventions may be new to you, and that's okay too - it's fun to learn about new things. Happy reading.

Chapter One:
Accidental Invention of Yummy Foods

"Food is everything we are.
It's an extension of nationalist feeling, ethnic feeling,
your personal history, your province, your region,
your tribe, your grandma.
It's inseparable from those from the get-go."
– Anthony Bourdain

1: Someone Left Their Lunch in the Sun Too Long

Have you ever seen those big semi-trucks pull into restaurant parking lots to unload food? Did you realize that both refrigeration and trucks are inventions of the past 200 years? Have you ever wondered how people used to transport food prior to modern technology?

Earliest people simply moved around like cattle, eating whatever they could find. If the berry bush had berries, they ate the berries on the spot. There was no putting things away for another day or transporting things from one place to another. Eventually, though, people began to farm; instead of them going to the food, the food came to them. People also began to domesticate other animals, such as dogs, to assist with the farming. Soon, they had domesticated animals for food too. Sheep were domesticated around 8000 B.C., and goats, cows, and buffalo followed shortly afterward.

Prior to modern technology, people often used the leak-proof stomachs of sheep and cattle to transport milk. In the Middle East, shepherds, for instance, might want to take milk with them so they could enjoy it while watching the sheep. Although the containers may have looked clean before adding the milk, they were not. Rennet, the enzyme used to make cheese, was naturally present in the stomachs of cud-chewing animals, and this included sheep, goats, cows, and buffalo, and, no matter how well the farmer tried to wash the vessel, traces of rennet were still in the vessel's lining.

Even though shepherds would leave the jugs under a shade tree or in a cave to keep the milk from heat, accidents were bound to happen. When the warm summer heat met the rennet in the stomach lining, it curdled the milk. An unknown shepherd got the nerve to taste this special form of curdled milk, and he liked what he tasted. Soon, people were deliberately curdling milk in these special rennet-lined jugs.

Shortly after that, people began straining the milk curds and then adding salt for preservation. Even with the salt, though, in the days before refrigeration the product was only good for a day. The shepherds called the tasty food "kwat", which meant "fermented". "Kwat" translates into an English word you will probably recognize . . . *cheese.*

2: One Person's Trash is Another Person's Treasure

Do you and your family take good care of your machines? Does your dad or mom change the car oil regularly? Do you reboot your computer periodically? Do you use surge protectors or unplug your television in an electrical storm? If you want the machine to last, you must take good care of it.

Edward Wilson believed in taking good care of his machines. In 1935, Edward was an employee of Flakall Corporation of Beloit, Wisconsin. His job was to make animal feed by sending corn through a grinder. To clean the grinder, moist corn was run through it from time to time. This cleaned the machine very well, but it also created a residue of airy corn blobs that had to be wiped away. It took only a few seconds to wipe the blobs, and, once the corn blobs were wiped, the machine was ready to create more animal food.

One day having wiped off the residue, Edward asked if he could take the corn blobs home with him. He was wondering how the blobs would taste and if they were even edible by humans. The company considered the residue to be trash, so they told him he could take as much as he wanted.

At his house, Edward tasted the cornball. It tasted good, but he thought it could be better, so he tried to add various spices to it. In time, he settled on a cheese flavor, named the product Korn Kurls, and shared the discovery with his boss at Flakall. His boss liked the Korn Kurl so much that he decided his company should make both the traditional animal food and this new human food. To make people feel better about the Korn Kurl, his boss changed the company name to Adams Foods.

The original corn curls came out of the machine as drippings, and, like snowflakes, no two were alike. Now that they were being mass produced, however, they came out of molds, so every piece had a consistent puff, curl, or ball shape.

Today, the corn products that are not flavored are called corn puffs or corn curls, and some people buy these corn products with no flavoring. Most people, though, like some flavoring to be sprinkled on their product; the flavored ones are known by both their sprinkled flavor and their shape. You probably know the most popular ones; they tend to leave a tale-telling orange residue on your fingers; we call them . . . *Cheese puffs/cheesy puffs, cheese curls, and cheese balls.*

3: Her Hopes Melted When the Chocolate Bar Didn't – But She'd Never Admit It

Do you like to impress people and be complimented on your work? Most people, including myself, do.

Ruth Wakefield was a people-pleaser too. Every night she had been baking butter cookies for her guests at The Toll House Inn, the bed-and-breakfast she and her husband Kenneth ran outside of Whitman, Massachusetts. Figuring her guests were as bored as she was with the routine, one night in 1937 she decided to add some baker's chocolate into the cookies. Much to her frustration, though, she found that she was out of baker's chocolate. Not one who quits, she found a Nestle chocolate bar, cut small chunks of chocolate from the bar, and placed the chunks into the cookie dough. She reasoned that the chocolate pieces would melt, adding a chocolate flavoring throughout the cookie. She took her cookie dough with the chocolate chunks added, cut it into cookie-sized balls, and then rolled out the balls. She placed the mixture on a cookie sheet in the oven and waited. In her mind, she could already hear people "oooing" and "ahhing" at the cookies.

Her dreams came crashing to a halt when she removed the cookies from the oven. The cookie dough itself was completely cooked; it was a delicious golden brown. However, the chocolate chunks had not melted, instead, they had simply gotten a little warm. She didn't have time to do another batch, so she brought out the cookies to the guests, pretending this was exactly what she had planned to cook all along. The guests didn't know any different, and they began to "ooo" and "ah" just as she had pictured them doing. (They weren't ooo-ing and ahh-ing to be polite; they were truly amazed.)

Ruth had cut up a Nestle chocolate bar, and so she reached out to Nestle to tell them what she had done and to offer them her recipe for them to print on their wrappers in exchange for a lifetime supply of chocolate. Nestle agreed, realizing this recipe could drive sales. Nestle even scored its candy bar so it would easily break into little pieces. The scored bar was not convenient enough for most people, though, so Nestle started selling little chips of chocolate that were already precut - they called these little chunks "morsels". Today, they still sell these small chunks, but now they are known as "chocolate chips."

The Toll House Inn dated back to 1791, when travelers came there to stay the night and pay their toll for using the road. Because of its historical background, the Toll House Inn was featured on the Betty Crocker radio show "Famous Foods from Famous Places" in 1939, and the Toll House Chocolate Crunch Cookie took center stage. That radio show made the cookie famous world-wide. Today, some places call the "Toll House Chocolate Crunch Cookie" the "Toll House Cookie", but most people know Ruth's invention as . . . **the chocolate chip cookie.**

4: The Search for the Holy Grail of Painkillers

Scars are a part of life. Perhaps you have a scar from where you fell off a bike? I have a scar from a hospital operation. Scars remind us of days gone by, and no matter how hard we try, that scar is always going to be with us for days and days to come.

Some scars heal and fade away; other scars hurt every day. Lieutenant Colonel John Pemberton had fought on the side of the Confederate States of America during the American Civil War and, at the Battle of Columbus in April 1865, he had received a saber wound to the chest. That wound had hurt him every day since then.

America had changed a lot twenty-one years after the end of the war, but each day John was reminded of that terrible battle that happened just days before the war ended. As with most soldiers of the Confederacy when the war ended, John was granted the freedom to return to his former occupation and to resume his career.

John was a pharmacist in Atlanta, and he had a good understanding of chemicals. For the past twenty-one years, he had been trying to blend the perfect combination of medicines to ease his pain. His goal was to find an opium-free painkiller, and his quest had led him to experiment with coca and cola wines. On May 6, he created a drink with a taste he had never experienced previously; he called it "Pemberton's French Wine Coca."

He was so in love with the taste that he wanted to share it, so he began to sell it at the soda fountain in his drug store. The drink went over well with the public, but alcohol addiction was becoming a problem in society. Pemberton realized if he was to sell the product, he would have to remove the alcohol and substitute something else. He kept the base syrup and blended it with carbonated water. He renamed the beverage after the two main ingredients, coca and cola, and called it Coca-Cola. The name was later changed again because some people were confusing "coca" for the drug cocaine and falsely claiming the soft drink had cocaine in it; today, we know the drink as . . . **Coke.**

5: When Life Gives You Stale Wheat, You Make . . .

Prior to 1880, people did not know much about the workings of the mind. If a person had a chemical imbalance, many people believed that the person had an evil spirit. Most people who were mentally ill could not hold jobs, and so they found themselves begging in the streets.

As society began to better understand mental health, the Church and concerned citizens wanted to help the mentally ill to recover and be productive citizens. John Harvey Kellogg and his brother Will Keith Kellogg were two of those people. They were Seventh Day Adventists who ran the Battle Creek Sanitarium, a mental health hospital, for their denomination in Battle Creek Michigan.

Running the sanitarium meant handling all aspects of daily activities, such as administrative paperwork and cooking. Officially, Will handled the business side and John handled the cooking, although in reality both did both jobs. John believed that diet greatly influenced the mind, so he was very particular about what his residents ate. He liked for them to eat bland foods because he believed bland foods relaxed the mind.

One day – August 8, 1894 to be exact, the brothers were cooking wheat for breakfast in the kitchen when a crisis arose, and they were needed elsewhere in the building. When they got back, they noticed the wheat had gone stale. Money was tight, so they tried to salvage the wheat by running it through rollers, hoping to turn the wheat into sheets of dough. When the wheat went through the rollers, though, it broke into flakes. Not giving up, they toasted the wheat flakes and served them to the residents. They called the flakes "granose."

The residents enjoyed eating the flaked wheat, and so the wheat flakes became a common menu item at the facility. Building on the success of the flaked wheat, John tried to recreate the process with corn. The process produced the same result, and in 1906, Will decided to mass market the corn product to the general public. He created the Battle Creek Toasted Corn Flake Company. The brothers had a falling out, though, when Will decided to add sugar to the bland flakes to improve their appeal; John believed sugared flakes were not true health food. Will also changed the name of the flakes from "granose" too; you may never have heard of "granose," but you have probably had a bowl of his flakey cereal . . . **Corn Flakes.**

6: The Best Thing Since Sliced Bread

Have you ever gotten distracted when you are trying to do something? For instance, maybe you are supposed to be working on a math worksheet, but that kid at the pencil sharpener is much more interesting, so you tend to focus on him?

Sylvester Graham noticed that boys tended to get distracted any time a girl would walk by them. Too, he noticed that the girls would get distracted if a boy walked by them. Sylvester didn't want people to distract each other, and he thought that one way to control it was through diet. He believed that certain foods made people more alert, to pay better attention, and to block out distractions.

Sylvester was a vegetarian, a person who never ate meat. He was a Presbyterian preacher as well, so he often offered dietary advice to the public. Sylvester lived in 1829 and processed foods, such as white bread, were just beginning to be mass produced. He believed that such bread was a problem for society, and that the ingredients within it were at least partially to blame for people's minds not functioning as he thought they should.

Sylvester saw that most people who bought the bread used it to make sandwiches. To discourage people from eating mass-produced bread, Sylvester developed a wheat-based cracker for them to put the sandwich ingredients on to eat. The cracker was bland and dry, but high in fiber. Sylvester believed this cracker was the secret to both good mental and physical health.

Sylvester's cracker is still healthy, but not as much as it was then – today, you can buy it with honey, sugar, cinnamon, and/or a lot of other things added to it. His cracker is often used in pie crusts and as the foundation for cheesecake. Campers like to melt candy bars and marshmallows between two of his crackers. We don't call the invention Sylvester's cracker today, though; we refer to it by his last name . . . **the Graham cracker.**

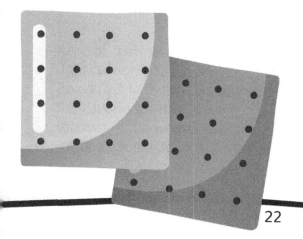

7: Menu Ronald

Has your mom ever bought a one-size-fits-all coat for you? I must have exceptionally long arms, because that one-size certainly does not fit me - at least not very well!

Prior to the 1970s, fast food was a one-size-fits-all assembly line. It didn't matter what your age was, you got the same size portion of food as everybody else did. One day in the mid-1970s, Yolanda Fernandez de Cofino, a Guatemala McDonald's worker, suggested that her store sell child-sized food portions to children. Her store took her up on the idea and developed the "Menu Ronald", a combination meal consisting of a burger, small fries, and a small sundae.

Word of the Menu Ronald got back to McDonald's headquarters in Chicago in the United States. The McDonald's leaders were suddenly aware that children were an overlooked market – children might not pay the bill, but they did influence where parents ate.

McDonald's hired Bob Bernstein to more fully develop Yolanda's accidental invention. Bob came up with a fancy box full of games; inside the box he placed a hamburger, small fries, and cookies, and he provided a soft drink. He also included a toy, such as an eraser shaped like Ronald McDonald. In 1977, he test marketed the concept in Kansas City, Missouri, and it was a big success. In 1979, it was released to all McDonald's restaurants.Soon other fast-food franchises were also trying to lure children.

McDonald's, though, sought to keep its customers. It added better and better toys. It allowed for chicken nuggets to be swapped for the burger. It offered healthier choices, such as milk instead of soda and apple wedges instead of fries.
Yolanda did not realize she was inventing something that would change the world when she invented the Menu Ronald – and you have probably not eaten a Menu Ronald, but you have likely eaten what Bob Bernstein named the invention . . . **the Happy Meal.**

8: The White Glove Experience

Have you ever borrowed somebody's pencil and then walked away with it, not even thinking about it not being yours? Then, when you realize that it is not yours – you "stole" it - you think about returning it, but, because you have gone so far from where you got it, you simply decide to return it the next time you are in the area? Be honest. Let me assure you, you are not the only one to borrow something and then forget to return it.

Anton Feuchtwanger was a sausage vendor at the 1904 World's Fair in St. Louis, Missouri. Anton specialized in hot sausages he called "frankfurters"; he named them after his birthplace in Frankfurt, part of Germany. Anton's sausages were piping hot, so he loaned white gloves to patrons to use while they ate his sausage so that they would not burn their hands. As you might suspect, people walked around the exhibits with their sausage, not even thinking about the fact that they needed to give the gloves back to Anton. Needless to say, Anton's glove supply began to run very low.

Gloves were expensive, and Anton was losing most of his profit. He considered charging a fee for the glove, but he realized that if he wanted to stay competitive with other food vendors, he could not charge his customers for gloves. The gloves were necessary, though; if he did not give his patrons gloves, they could not enjoy his food and would not buy from him. What was he to do? It sounded like a situation in which there was no good answer.

Anton suddenly realized that although people needed something to hold his sausage, no one said it had to be a glove. His brother-in-law was a baker, and together they created a long roll that would fit the meat. Anton cut a slit in each roll and inserted the sausage. The rolls were a success; people thought they were a novelty and flocked to his booth to try one.

Today, many companies make those long rolls. Some put the cut at the top; others put it at the side. People often add condiments to the sausage; different regions of the world like different condiments. I personally like ketchup, mustard, relish, and onion, but some people like sauerkraut, peppers, mayonnaise, cheese, and numerous other sauces. Frankfurters go by several names, including franks, wieners, and hotdogs. Anton may have called his invention a roll, but today we know that bread we put hotdogs on as . . . **the hotdog bun.**

9: Someone Didn't Bring Enough Dishes

Do you remember a time in school where the student next to you needed a pencil? Maybe their pencil broke; maybe they just forgot to bring one. Did you help them out? Maybe you have even been the kid who forgot your pencil; do you remember how grateful you were to the person who gave you one?

Ernest Hamwi was a Syrian vendor selling waffle-like pastries called "zalabis" at the 1904 World's Fair in St. Louis, Missouri. In the booth next to his booth was a man who was selling ice-cream. If you have ever been in Missouri in the summer, you know that it is hot and muggy, and so ice-cream was selling fast. In fact, it was selling so fast that the ice-cream vendor ran out of bowls. Without bowls, he could not make any sales, and he was going to miss out on a lot of potential income.

Hamwi saw the need and realized he was in the position to help. He approached the vendor and shared his idea. He proposed rolling a zalabis into a cornucopia shape to serve as a dish. (Cornucopias are those "horns of plenty" that you often see at Thanksgiving holding fruit and other decorations.) The ice-cream vendor was receptive to the idea; serving it in a waffle was better than not serving it at all.

Hamwi made a special zalabis and folded it. After the cornucopia cooled for a few seconds, the vendor set a scoop of ice-cream on top of the cornucopia. If either gentleman had a doubt that waffles and ice cream would not go well together, he was wrong. The people at the fair loved it and, thanks to Hamwi, the ice cream vendor was able to satisfy all his potential customers.

Hamwi knew he had found a new use for his product and set about manufacturing them. In time, the product diversified. The waffle cornucopia remained popular, but people also liked a battered product from a specifically designed mold that held the ice cream level. The waffle ice-cream holder was called the cornucopia for a couple of years, but, in time, people began to call both types of edible ice-cream holders the name we know them by today . . . **the ice-cream cone.**

10: A Taste of Wrath

Do you have a favorite food? Most people do.

Thornton Prince was a handsome African American man living in Nashville, Tennessee, who loved fried chicken. One night his girlfriend went over to his house and made him his favorite dish. When Thornton didn't come home on time - he didn't even call, she was furious. She was so angry she put all the hottest spices she could find on his chicken. It still looked like ordinary chicken, but she knew it sure wouldn't taste like it.

Thornton eventually found his way home. He greeted his girlfriend with a kiss as if nothing was wrong and then sat down to eat. When he bit into the chicken, his mouth was on fire, just as she thought it would be – and - here is where she was wrong - he loved it. He liked it so much that he asked for the recipe – in all seriousness, he wanted the recipe. When she couldn't remember the exact details, he experimented, trying to recreate the same amount of each ingredient that she had used.

Thornton finally found a recipe close to it, and he wanted to share it with the world. Thornton knew that fried chicken establishments dotted the South, but he believed his recipe was different because of the chili and cayenne peppers. In fact, he had so much confidence that the recipe would be a hit that he opened Prince's Fried Chicken Shack in the 1930s in Nashville, Tennessee.

Lots of everyday people dropped by, and even some country music celebrities dined in his restaurant. The restaurant was able to survive over the years, but the restaurant and the recipe never took off – until 2007. In 2007, Nashville Mayor Bill Purcell fell in love with the recipe. He liked it so much that he came to the restaurant regularly, and he even started a town-wide Hot Chicken Festival. Spicy chicken soon became a nationwide and worldwide fad, with large chains such as O'Charley's and KFC serving it. Today, Prince's restaurant ships fried chicken literally around the world.

You may never have been to Nashville to taste Thornton's exact spicy recipe, but you have likely tried a generic version of it. Just as hamburgers come in a variety of ways, so does spicy chicken; in fact, as noted earlier, Thornton himself tried numerous combinations before settling on what he considered the perfect blend of spices. Thornton created spicy chicken in 1930; but spicy chicken doesn't go by the name "spicy chicken"; it goes by a name you are likely more familiar with. . . **Nashville Hot Chicken.**

11: It's Cheesy but It's True

Most of us have "the usual." When you go to a restaurant, do you order something new, or do you stick with "the usual." Most of the time we like what has worked in the past - but occasionally we do seek a change.

Mamie Finan was in a rut. Mamie was a regular patron of the Victory Club in Peidrs Negras, Coahuila, Mexico, across the border from Texas– she had been ordering the same food day after day. Tired of the same foods, she asked the chef, Ignacio Anaya Garcia, to create a new dish for her and her three friends. He accepted the challenge, having no idea of exactly what he was going to do.

He went back into the kitchen and spotted corn chips. He looked around for something else to go with them and saw jalapeno peppers. He took the fresh corn chips, poured them on a plate, sliced jalapeno peppers on them, and then smothered the chips and peppers with melted cheese. He then brought it out to the women. The women were pleased with the presentation; the dish looked delicious. But was it? The women hesitantly tried it; they loved the combination. When asked what the dish was called, Ignacio said, "Nacho's Special" referencing the fact that he made it. (In Spanish, his name "Ignacio" translates into "Nacho")

When the restaurant owner saw how well the women liked the dish, he put the dish on the menu. Nachos were very popular, and people began to request other ingredients on the chips and peppers as well; you may have had them with black beans, sour cream, onions, banana peppers, guacamole, and black olives. Nachos quickly became a regional food, making their way to Los Angeles and then to Texas. Nachos might have remained a regional dish if it hadn't been for a sportscaster.

Baseball stadiums are known for hotdogs, but they also serve other food as well. With its three ingredients of corn chips, peppers, and cheese, nachos could be fixed quickly, and, because they were popular in the region, they were on the menu at Arlington Stadium in Dallas, Texas, in 1974. While broadcasting a Monday Night Football game from Dallas, Texas, Howard Cosell, a famous broadcaster at the time, tried the stadium's nachos for the first time. He liked them so much that he raved about them on the air for everyone across the nation to hear. After that, nachos became very popular not just in Mexico but in the United States and then the rest of the world. Howard Cosell had taught a generation words like "touchdown" and on this night he introduced another word into the nation's vocabulary, a word that he himself had not heard until that day... *the word "nachos."*

12: An Icy Treat

Have you ever thought, "I've got to have a drink. I've got to have a drink," and that is all you can think about - getting that drink. However, once you get that drink and you see your friends, then suddenly that drink that was so important no longer matters? That's what happened to Frank Epperson too.

Eleven-year-old Frank Epperson was thirsty one San Francisco afternoon in 1905, so he got himself a glass of water. Water itself is bland, as you know, so he added some soda powder to give it flavor. He stirred the mixture with a wooden stick and was just about to have a sip when he saw his friends up the road. Not wanting to miss an adventure, he set down his drink and ran up the street to join them.

An unusual thing happened in San Francisco that night – the temperature dropped below freezing. It's not unheard of for San Francisco to be that cold, but it is very rare. The rare cold spell was a big surprise, and nobody was more surprised than Frank Epperson. You see, in his hurry to be with his friends, Frank had forgotten his drink, and it sat outside in the freezing temperature all night. The next day when Frank went outside to play, he happened to see the drink - It was frozen like a rock.

Frank went to the kitchen and ran warm water on the side of the glass, breaking the ice inside free. He grabbed the ice by the wooden stick and pulled it out. Being curious as to how it would taste, he held onto the stick and licked the flavored ice. He liked the treat so much that he decided to deliberately make more of them to sell in the neighborhood. Instead of calling the flavored ice on a stick an icicle, he named it the Epsicle after himself. Epsicle, though, is not the name we know that treat by today.

In 1923, Frank decided to patent the idea; he did not want anybody to steal his idea. He was 29 years-old now, and he had kids of his own. He asked his children what they thought the flavored ice treat should be called. One of them suggested using the term "pop", because "pop" was slang for "dad," a reminder their dad was the inventor. Frank realized "pop" was also a reminder of the soda powder, for soda is known in some parts of the United States as "pop". He went with that suggestion. Today we call that delicious, flavored ice on a wooden stick . . . ***the popsicle.***

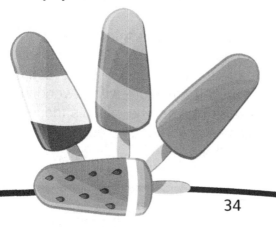

13: The Cook Had a Chip on His Shoulder

Have you ever met someone who just could not seem to be pleased? No matter what you did, they still weren't happy. When you ask them what they wanted, they couldn't describe it; they just knew it is not what you had done so far. They kept telling you to try again.

George Crum, a cook at Moon's Lake House in the resort town of Saratoga Springs, New York, was dealing with such a customer on August 24, 1853. The customer had ordered hand-cut French fries, a dish the restaurant called Moon's Home Cooked Potatoes. George had fulfilled the order, but the customer had sent the fries back because they were too soggy. George had then cooked a new batch of fries just for that customer and brought them out to him. Instead of being told thank you, he was told they were too salty, and the French fry critic asked him to try again. George willingly went back to the kitchen, cut some more fries, cooked them, and came out with a third batch. This batch too was met with displeasure also; the patron declared they were cut too thick.

"Too thick?" Crum muttered in frustration as he walked the plate of fries back to the kitchen. "Too thick?" he muttered again, grabbing his paring knife and a potato. He proceeded to cut several potatoes extremely thin, fried them until they were overly crisp, and then seasoned them with extra salt. "Let's see how you like these," he muttered, put on a fake smile, and carried the dish to the picky patron. He was angry, and he expected the customer to try the dish and be repulsed by the paper thinness, the extra crispness, and the extra saltiness. To his surprise, the patron loved them.

Word about the thin potatoes traveled quickly, for, you see, the picky patron was Cornelius Vanderbilt, a railroad tycoon. By 1860, Crum had his own lakeside restaurant, Crum's House. He branded his creation the Saratoga Chip, and that brand is still in operation today. If you haven't had a Saratoga Chip, you have likely enjoyed a competitor's version of his thinly sliced potato; George called it the Saratoga Chip, but we know his invention as . . . **the potato chip.**

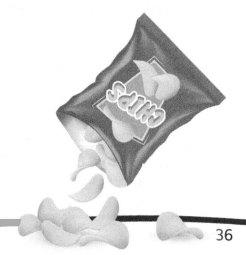

14: Respect the Runt

Have you ever been the runt of the group? I know I have. (I have been the runt when hanging out with the older neighborhood boys; but the group leader when with my cousins.) As the runt, I got pushed aside. The people who were stronger than me or had more powerful friends than me, such as the tomboy up the street the boys all wanted to impress, would elbow me out of the way, take what they wanted, and then leave the rest -if anything at all - for me. Although bullying behavior is frowned upon in our culture, bullying still exists. I suspect you too have been bullied, although most of us don't like to talk about it.

Bullying is nothing new; bullying existed in past cultures too. Bullying is probably responsible for some of the accidental discoveries that were made. For instance, almost 4000 years ago around 2000 BC, a group of children left the primitive campsite in search of treasure. The kids would not have had bikes like many children in our culture; they would have hiked. As they hiked on this particular day, one of them found a grape vine full of luscious grapes. He called his friends to come see. The friends verified it was indeed a grapevine, and then tasted one of the grapes. It was delicious. The other children also wanted to taste. They shoved the runt of the group to the ground, ate grapes until they were full, and then started back to their camp. As they started to walk away, they told the runt that he could eat at last.

The runt had worked up quite an appetite watching the other children eat. When he got to the grape vine, though, he saw that it had been picked clean. There were no plump purple grapes for him. The greedy children had eaten them all. All that was left were some shriveled up grapes.

Deciding something was better than nothing, he bit into the shriveled grape. It was delicious! Wanting to share his joy, he called to his friends, "Come back, everybody. You left the best part." (We runts don't hold grudges, and, having experienced bullying ourselves, we try never to bully other people.) His friends came back, and he offered them some of the shriveled grapes.

As civilization moved from hunting-and-gathering to farming, people began to grow vineyards full of the best grapes imaginable. They ate the grapes, they turned the grapes into wine, and – yes – they even allowed some of the grapes to shrivel on the vine. Today, these shriveled grapes are usually put into boxes. Sometimes they are consumed directly from the box, and other times they are placed in salads, used as a beverage flavoring, or turned into a sauce for a ham. We usually don't think of them as shriveled grapes, though; we call them . . . *raisins.*

15: The Great Depression Offered a Great Opportunity

Have you ever had something you really liked and then lost it? Losing it made you sad, didn't it? This is how many people felt during the Great Depression in the United States, tough times that began in 1929 and went through the 1930s. Many people who had lots of money in the 1920s now found that they had little money; people who could afford luxuries could barely afford essentials. Many people even had to do without many essentials. People were, pardon the pun, depressed.

Now, imagine that there was a beverage that you could drink to take away that feeling of depression and make you feel accepting of the situation and optimistic about the future; how would you feel? Would you want to try it? Charles Leiper Grigg claimed to have made such a drink. Charles had actually launched the drink two weeks before the Great Stock Market Crash, but, because of his job in advertising, he saw a need to rebrand the product. Charles was not lying when he rebranded it, claiming his drink could make a person feel more relaxed; the lemon lime soda that he was introducing contained lithium citrate, a mood-stabilizing drug. He called the beverage Bib-Label Lithiated Lemon-Lime soda.

Charles was an advertiser who sold beverages for soda companies, but his real passion was creating and selling his own sodas. In the 1920s Charles had tried to sell an orange soda, but his brand Howdy had gotten crushed – yes, that's a pun referring to Orange Crush - by the competition. When great prosperity followed World War II in the United States, the market for a drink to make one feel relaxed dried up. Charles realized another rebranding was in order. In 1948 he removed the lithium citrate from the beverage, and he promoted the beverage as a refreshing lemon lime drink. It was clearly the right decision, for his beverage is still selling well today.

Being a marketer, he had known that the name Bib-Label Lithiated Lemon-Lime soda was too stuffy to sell many drinks, so he renamed it 7-Up Lithiated Lemon Soda. (No one knows where the name came from; it may have been that seven key ingredients were in the mixture.) In 1936, he shortened the name to the name you know it as today . . . **7-Up.**

Chapter Two:
Accidental Invention of Toys

"To this day,
I have the most fond memories of some of my old toys."
~ Michael Keaton

16: Everything's Peachy

Have you ever gone to one of those you-pick farms? When you get there, you are given a wooden basket or a wooden tub – your choice – and then you go into the orchard to fill your tub with what the farm grows - apples, peaches, cherries, and strawberries, for instance. You can pick things that have fallen to the ground; you can pick things directly off the tree. You are charged by the tub, so you can pick as many as will fit in the tub and you can make sure that you get only the ones that you like. Did you know that those wooden tubs inspired an accidental invention? It's true; they did. James Naismith was a graduate student at Springfield College in Massachusetts. He was asked to come up with a game that the students could play inside during the winter months. In December of 1891, he came up with basketball - that's right, basketball.

The game he designed was more like rugby than the basketball of today. Each team had nine players, and the goal of the game was to put the soccer ball into the opponent's goal. Naismith found a soccer ball, but he didn't find any goals – so he resorted to using peach baskets. He literally nailed a peach basket at each end of the gym. The early games were very low scoring, but should a goal be made, a timeout was called while someone got on a ladder and got the ball down.

The game spread quickly, first through the YMCA (Young Men's Christian Association) and then colleges. The first public game was in 1892; the first game between colleges was 1895. Professional basketball began in 1898. Today, basketball is played worldwide, and it is even an event at the summer Olympics.

In 1905, seven years after professional basketball had begun, the peach baskets were replaced. The baskets did not let the ball fall through the bottom, and they took great abuse from the ball striking them. In their stead was the modern version of his peach basket; Naismith accidently created . . . *the basketball hoop, backboard, and net.*

17: Pie in the Sky

Have you ever seen something but not really seen something? For instance, have you walked up a flight of steps recently? You likely saw all the steps; can you tell me how many steps there were? If you can't, don't feel bad. Most people see, but they do not observe. Those who observe sometimes state the obvious, and, because no one else has thought to observe it, they get recognized as the inventor. Consider the case of Fred Morrison.

Fred Morrison lived in Bridgeport, Connecticut, the home of Yale University and of the Frisbie Pie company. Have you ever heard of the Frisbie Pie company? If not, let me take a moment to inform you. William Frisbie started selling pies in Bridgeport, Connecticut in 1871 from his home. His pies were very popular, and by 1915 he was operating a three-story bakery downtown.

He served his pie in tins that were marked Frisbie Pies, and, after the pie was consumed, parents sometimes gave the children the pie tins to play with. By turning the pie tin upside down and then flinging it, the saucer would glide through the air smoothly. The children would throw the tins to each other as if they were flying saucers from Mars. Children weren't the only one's throwing the pie tins, though. Employees of the Frisbie Pie Company often threw the plates to each other. Even college students, such as those on Bridgeport's Yale college campus, were doing it.

One day Fred Morrison saw the Yale college students playing with the tin discs everyone considered to be pieces of trash, throwing them to each other and playing various games with them. He observed them playing catch, playing keep-away, playing American football, having contests to see who could fly it the greatest distance, and having contests to see who could land it on a particular line. Fred didn't just see them playing; Fred observed them playing.

Fred realized that the flying disc had potential as a toy. He created a plastic version of the tin plate and the toy company Wham-o sold the first one in 1957. Ed Headrick, a Wham-o employee, added raised rings to the flying disk to stabilize its flight; the Rings of Headrick are named after him. Fred called his invention the "Pluto Platter," but, in 1958, Wham-o renamed it. Wham-o wanted to stir up memories of its roots, so Wham-o modified the spelling but not the pronunciation of the name that was printed on all the pie tins; to this day, we still call the product . . . *the Frisbee.*

18: A Rock Concert Changed This from Military Equipment into a Toy

Ever been to a concert, a fair, or a picnic and seen people wave those glow-in the dark wands in the air? Many times, those wands can be bent and then locked to form necklaces and bracelets, creating mysterious circles that can be seen from far away. Believe it or not, this popular children's toy did not begin as a toy.

These glowing sticks were created in the 1960s, but did not become popular as a children's toy until the late 1970s. Fluorescent, glow-in-the-dark paint had been created in 1933, but the concept of using it in a stick did not come about until the 1960s. The glowing wand was created when Edwin Chandross of Bell Labs realized that by placing chemicals in each side of the tube and then breaking the barrier between them, the chemicals would react and create a light which could then be reflected through the tube. Today's sticks contain two chemicals, peroxide, and fluorophore, which, when brought together, create a glow that lasts for several hours.

The U.S. military saw lots of potential uses for the tube, and, beginning in 1973, began to purchase the tubes. The tubes had much that the military liked about them: They were light to carry, and they stored well; the light they produced lasted for hours; they were relatively cheap; and they required no batteries. By laying them in a field, paratroopers could see where they were to touch down, airplanes could see where to land, and gunners could see their target.

The product was made at American Cyanamid. One day one of the factory worker's children snuck some sticks into his backpack and took them to a Grateful Dead concert. During the show at the Yale Ball in New Haven, Connecticut, he took out the sticks and passed them down to his new-found friends at the concert. He showed them how to bend the stick so that the barrier inside was broken and the stick began to glow. Soon, he and those around him were waving the sticks like they wouldwave a flag. That evening, people talked more about the sticks than about the band!

The idea of waving the stick as if it were an Independence Day sparkler caught on fast. Factory management began to recognize the non-military use of these sticks. Today, these man-made sticks that look like lit-up fireflies come in a variety of colors – neon yellow, neon pink, neon blue, blue-green, and neon green, to name a few. The sticks are readily available year-round; you can buy them at the local dollar-store. You will find them at many children's birthday parties and being passed out at Halloween. Parents use them for both a toy and as a safety device, for when children wear them drivers can easily see them. This stick with a glow has a very appropriate name; you have likely heard it called . . . *the Glow Stick.*

19: The Inventors Were as Flexible as the Putty They Created

Do you keep up with current events? It is important to know what is happening around town, around the nation, and around the globe. Being in the know helps you to realize opportunities that are around you.

Kay Zufall was a nursery schoolteacher who kept up on current events. One day in the late 1950s she read that children were making art projects from a wallpaper cleaning putty. If it hadn't been for her making this observation of an accidental invention, the invention probably would have gone unnoticed.

Kay was the sister-in-law to Joseph McVicker, who was the nephew of Noah McVicker, the man who had come up with the wallpaper cleaning putty the children were using. Noah had been working at a soap making company in the early 1930s, when the company was approached by Kroger Grocery to make a cleaning product to remove coal residue from the wallpaper. Noah had come up with a product that did exactly that - putty that could be rolled over a stain and remove the stain, and Kroger had sold lots of it. However, in the late 1940s, washable vinyl wallpaper had been created, and nobody needed Noah's cleaning product.

Now, though, Kay realized people did need Noah's product. She suggested that Noah and Joseph make the product and sell it as a toy putty for children. They agreed to do it, forming the Rainbow Crafts Company in 1956. They sold their first putty in 1957; it was an off-white color. Soon they were selling directly to schools and to department stores. By the end of the year, they were offering red, yellow, and blue colors in addition to white.

You may never have known the product started as a cleaning product, but you probably have enjoyed playing with the dough-like putty. Joseph recognized the doughiness to the product and renamed the putty in 1956 to what you likely know it as . . . *Play Doh.*

20: Finding Its Niche

None of us like to be rejected. We all want to be accepted. Rejection is a part of life. I remember when my dad applied for a job and he got back a rejection letter that said, "We know you are going to be the perfect fit somewhere . . . it's just not here." My dad took the message to heart, found his niche, and is very happy.

James Wright also got rejected. During World War II, the United States government had asked James, an employee of General Electric, to create a rubber substitute. James did exactly that, creating "Nutty Putty" from boric acid and silicone oil in 1942, but the government said that it was too close to what other people had already invented and that they were sorry but that they could not use his invention.

James could have given up when he heard this, but, in 1943, he decided to see if his product – a rubber-like substance that could bounce and stretch – had selling potential as a novelty toy. He kept trying for the next five years, but the product's sales were dismal. However, one of the people who decided to carry his product in 1948 was the owner of a toy store called The Block Shop, and the person assigned to market the toy in the Block Shop's Christmas catalog was Peter Hodgson. The owner of the toy store renamed "Nutty Putty" as "Bouncing Putty" for the toy store that Christmas; Peter saw potential in the toy he was marketing, so shortly after Christmas he borrowed money and bought the rights to the product from James.

As a marketer, Peter knew how to get the word out and how to make the product look attractive. He arranged for the *New Yorker* magazine to run an article about his product. Also, he knew Easter was coming, so he decided to place the putty in a red plastic egg. He also changed the name from Nutty Putty to something else – I'll tell you about that in a minute. Believe it or not, he sold over 250,000 eggs in three days and over six million his first year. Being a toy was the perfect fit! Marketing made a difference, but the toy lived up to its hype, and continues to appear in store toy aisles today. We no longer call it "Nutty Putty" or "Bouncing Putty", we call it . . . *Silly Putty.*

21: A Bright Idea

Ever have a good idea and share it? Once it's out there, my guess is people try to improve upon it. They add to it, they tweak it, the substitute parts, and do other things all in the name of making it better. Even the best ideas, such as Thomas Edison's lightbulb, got tweaked.

A surgeon asked Erwin Perzy, the owner of a medical supply business outside Vienna, Austria in 1900 to make Thomas Edison's lightbulb brighter. The surgeon thought Edison's bulb was too dull to do surgery under; he needed one with a much greater wattage.

Perzy accepted the challenge. He placed a glass-globe in front of a candle to increase the light's magnification. Then, he sprinkled glitter into the globe to increase the brightness. The glitter sank too quickly, so he emptied the globe and tried semolina flakes (found in baby food). This too failed.

Perzy, though, was fascinated with the result. The small white particles were drifting aimlessly in the globe; it looked like it was snowing in the globe. He was so impressed that he decided to make and sell these globes of fake snow. By 1905, he had established Firm Perzy, where he produced these globes full of snow-like material. Inside the globe he had small pewter church figurines. By turning the globe upside down and then setting it down, the viewer could watch a gentle snow fall on the pewter figures. He called his accidental invention Schneekugel, but you know it by its English name . . . *the Snow Globe.*

22: Springing to Fame

Ever knock something off a shelf and all you can do is sit there in horror watching it fall and waiting for it to hit the floor? What is happening in a matter of seconds feels like it is happening over many minutes; the whole world appears to be in slow motion. Finally, at long last, you hear the BANG that confirms the item has hit the floor.

Richard James, a naval engineer in World War II, had that kind of moment. He was working with torsion springs - the kind of spring found in clothes pins, mouse traps, and garage doors - when one fell out of a box. He watched in awe as it moved gracefully head-over-tail again and again, snaking its way to the floor.

Richard was so impressed with what he saw that day that he wanted to create it so he could see it again – he had never seen a walking spring before that day, and he hadn't seen one since. He finally came up with a compressed coil – 80 feet of wire compressed into a two-inch space – and attempted to sell it to toy stores, but toy sellers were quick to point out that the grey spring was not colorful nor was the crawling snake noisy as it walked. Toy sellers believe a toy needed to be colorful and noisy to grab children's attention - and Richard's accidental invention was neither, so no one took up the opportunity to sell his springy snake.

Although toy makers had their doubts about his product, Richard believed the product was fun and that kids of all ages would find that it was too. When the professionals turned him down, Richard arranged his own product demonstrations. His big break came in the Christmas season of 1945 at the Gimbels Department Store in Philadelphia. In less than three minutes, he sold 400 products and he has since sold 300 million. Do you know the name of this snake-like product? His wife came up with the name for this product because of the way it slinked downstairs without making hardly a sound . . . **The Slinky.**

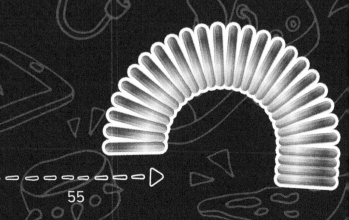

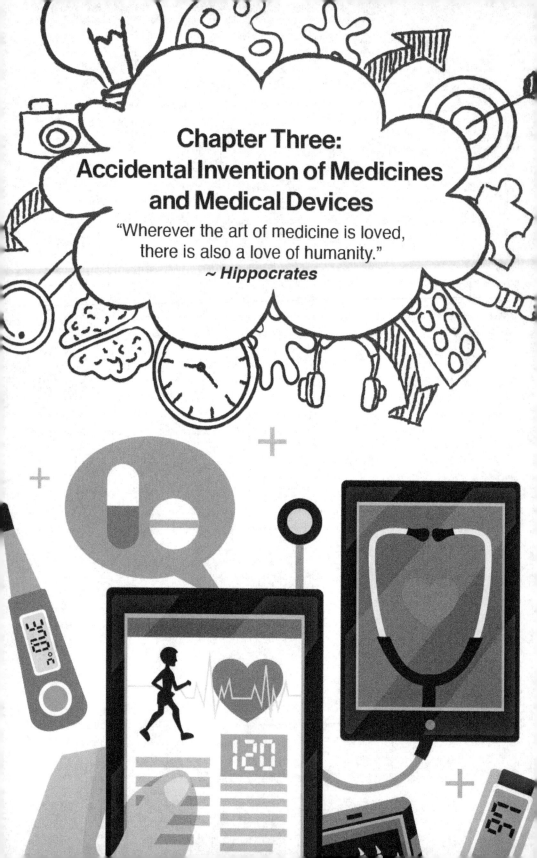

Chapter Three:
Accidental Invention of Medicines and Medical Devices

"Wherever the art of medicine is loved,
there is also a love of humanity."
~ *Hippocrates*

23: Everything is Funny Until Somebody Gets Hurt

Has your mom ever let you place the spout of a helium balloon in your mouth, allowed you to inhale, and then listened to you talk? (My mom would not let me do that, but a lot of my friends' moms let them.) After inhaling the helium from the balloon, the person talked in a real high-pitched voice. Try as hard as they might, they could not speak in their normal voice until the helium was out of their system.

Beginning in the 1790s and going through the first half of the nineteenth century, the fad at adult high-society parties was to inhale nitrous oxide; whereas helium makes you talk in a squeaky voice, nitrous oxide makes you laugh uncontrollably. Having sucked nitrous oxide, people howled with laughter, and most enjoyed both the experience of laughing as well as seeing their friends making fools of themselves. Humphry Davy, according to one story, was one of those people who inhaled the nitrous oxide. He was a British surgeon's apprentice. He realized that the gas did indeed make him laugh but it also numbed him to pain, something no one else had noticed. He was a surgeon, and, after his experience with nitrous oxide, he often used this "laughing gas" to numb his patients.

Horace Wells had a similar experience in 1844. He was a dentist. One of the people at the party he attended injured himself while on nitrous oxide; the man had a deep cut in his leg but didn't care. The man just kept laughing and laughing. Luckily, Horace knew how serious the injury was, kept his composure, and gave the man the help he needed. Horace realized that nitrous oxide not only made people laugh, but it also made people oblivious to pain; that was something a dentist could appreciate. He began to use "laughing gas" on his patients.

In summary, a surgeon and a dentist both came across "laughing gas" as an adult toy; something adults did at gatherings for fun. They both, though, saw its unrealized effect of making people numb to pain. Today, we don't call it and similar agents that make us numb to pain "laughing gas" anymore, we call them . . . *anesthesia.*

What would you do for your parents if they were sick? Would you sell your favorite possession so they could go to the doctor? Would you give them all the time that you could? When you truly love somebody, you will do anything for them.

Felix Hoffmann truly loved his dad. Felix Hoffmann's dad was suffering from arthritis. The arthritis was so bad that it hurt for his dad to move his joints in ways that we take for granted. He couldn't bend his fingers without great pain; it hurt to move his arms. Felix wanted to help his dad, and he was willing to do anything for him.

Felix worked for Bayer, a German chemical company that worked on medicines. Most medicines come from plant roots and tree bark, and their history goes back to very early human societies. People from early societies knew that willow tree bark helped relieve pain; however, they also knew the human stomach could not take a large dose of it. In the 1800s, scientists had concluded that it was the chemical salicin in the bark that did the soothing. Scientists had been able to isolate the salicin in 1829, but it was too rough on one's stomach to take. In 1853, French chemist Charles Gerhardt, though, had found a way to make the salicin takeable by mixing it with other chemicals; Charles, though, had thought it was not worth the time to make the drug. Felix came across Charles's notes, including his recipe for making salicin acceptable to the human body.

Felix was desperate. His dad needed his help. He followed Charles's recipe and cooked up a batch of the compound. He then took it to his dad. His dad was able to ingest it, and, shortly thereafter, felt like a brand-new person. Felix believed he had found the wonder drug.

Charles had had no desire to market the product; Felix was so excited he couldn't wait to market it. He convinced Bayer to sell the wonder drug. Bayer patented the drug in 1900. Today, the drug is still used for arthritis, but most people use it as a blood thinner and as a headache remedy. You may not have even known the product was good for arthritis, but you probably knew the product was good for headaches; you know this product as . . . **Aspirin.**

Something on the threads!

Has a secret ever changed your life? You got along fine without knowing about it, but, once you knew about it, it impacted everything you did? When you come across an invention, it is much like coming across a secret – your world changes. Some inventions are more discoveries than inventions; however, the effect is still the same – the accident led to the previously unknown item becoming known and that knowledge changed daily life.

Antonie van Leeuwenhoek began his career at the age 16 as an apprentice to a textile merchant in 1648. (An apprenticeship is on-the-job training; most people call it an internship today.) Among his duties was to be the inspector of quality; his job was to look under the microscope at the fabric to be purchased to count the number of threads to ensure that the thread count was accurate because his boss didn't want to buy clothing that was not up to standards.

Antonie enjoyed science and liked to invent. Working at this job in textiles was likely the first time he had seen a microscope. Antonie invented a stronger lens which allowed him to see the fibers in even more detail; over his life, Antony would invent 500 different microscopes.

One day as Antonie peered into the microscope and looked at the threads, he saw tiny microorganisms. He thought at first his eyes were playing tricks, but they really were tiny, microscopic, rod-shaped, single cell beings living on the clothing. Antonie shared his discovery with other scientists; they did not believe him at first, but, once they saw the microorganisms for themselves, they believed him.

Antonie later became the first person to see red blood cells. Today, he is regarded as the father of the field of microbiology. Those rod-shaped organisms that he saw, his accidental invention so-to-speak, changed the world of medicine. Antony named the rod-shaped beings after the Latin word for "rod" . . . *bacteria.*

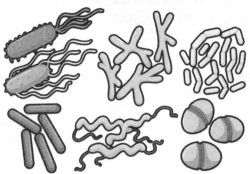

Have you ever tried to fix a row of Christmas lights? If one light is bad, the whole string goes bad. To fix it, you can take one light out, put in a good one, and see if the lights come on. If they do, you know that the light you removed was the bad bulb; if they don't come on, you know to put the old bulb back in and then move on to try replacing the next bulb.

That is like how science works as well. Science tries to isolate one thing, and, if things change, that isolated item is determined to be the cause. Oskar Minkowski and Josef von Mering were two scientists who were trying to understand how the pancreas affects digestion in 1889. To see if the pancreas was the cause of digestion, they removed the pancreas from an otherwise healthy dog.

When they went to check on the dog a couple of days later, they heard a strange buzzing sound coming from the dog's area. They looked at each other in puzzlement and proceeded to the dog's cage. It might take a scientist to figure out why it was happening, but anyone could figure out what was happening - flies, lots and lots of flies, were buzzing around the dog's urine. You may not realize it but flies normally don't buzz around urine. Oscar and Josef knew they had a mystery on their hands.

When they tested the urine, they found that it was full of excessive sugar. They concluded that by removing the pancreas, they had affected the dog's ability to regulate sugar. They realized that the pancreas somehow helped to control one's sugar. They concluded that when the pancreas did not work right or was not there to work, one's sugar got out of control.

Fred Banting and Charles Best, a professor and his student at the University of Toronto, continued Oscar and Josef's work. They studied the pancreas and realized that the pancreas secreted insulin, and that insulin was what controlled the body's blood sugar. Upon further research, they realized they could help people with diabetes whose body did not produce enough of the chemical to neutralize sugar by injecting them with doses of insulin. What began as a scientific investigation of the digestive process led to the discovery of the chemical that regulates sugar. You may know of someone with diabetes who has to take shots of this accidental invention since their body is not creating enough of it on its own; Oscar and Josef, along with Fred and Charles, invented . . . *insulin.*

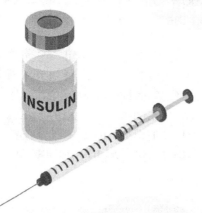

27: "There's Something in Your Eye"

Have you ever heard the expression that something good is going to come out of something bad? For the optimistic people, no matter how dark a cloud is, there is a silver lining. Optimists believe there is good to be seen in every bad situation.

Gordon Cleaver was lucky he saw it all. He was a pilot in the Royal Air Force during World War II, and, during an attack, he had experienced a small piece of plastic going into his eye. He was examined the day it happened by Dr. Nicholas Ridley, an eye specialist. Dr. Ridley decided it best to leave the plastic in the eye unless a major problem developed. Dr. Ridley continued to monitor Gordon even after the war was over. Fortunately, the plastic did not move and did not do further damage.

Realizing that the piece of plastic in Gordon's eye was not hurting him and nor was it being rejected by his body, Dr. Ridley decided to implant a plastic lens into a cataract patient, Harold Ripley, immediately after he removed Harold's cataract on November 29, 1949. If Gordon Cleaver could live with a piece of plastic in his eye, why couldn't Harold Ripley live with a plastic lens in his eye? The operation was a success.

Many people were concerned with this type of eye surgery when it first began, and it was slow to gain acceptance. Since the 1970s, though, millions of such surgeries have been performed and little controversy surrounds the procedure today. For some people, having the plastic lens put into their eye is an alternative to both contacts and glasses. If you ever need the procedure to improve your vision, you will want to remember that the little piece of plastic that Dr. Ridley developed and inserted is known as . . . *the intraocular lens.*

28: He Wasn't Your Average Joe

Have you ever noticed that people like to name things after people they respect? For instance, both "Washington, D.C." and Washington state are both named after George Washington, the first President of the United States. Similarly, Columbus, Ohio and Columbia, South Carolina are named after the explorer Christopher Columbus. Towns, streets, objects, and even people are named after people we respect.

Joseph Lawrence was a big fan of Joseph Lister. In 1860, Louis Pasteur had come up with a theory that microscopic bacteria were in the air, and the technology to see such bacteria under the microscope had been invented. As with most scientific theories, this one had its sceptics, but Joseph Lister was not one of them. Joseph Lister believed Pasteur's claims, and, as a British surgeon, he took the theory and put it into practice. Before his next surgery, Lister sprayed the air of the surgery room to try to kill any bacteria. As he operated, he continued to have the air cleansed of bacteria. The survival rate of Lister's surgical patients was far greater than average, and his steps have become second-nature to all doctors.

Joseph Lawrence wanted to invent an antiseptic that would kill germs that people like Joseph Lister could spray during surgeries. He created one in 1879, and in 1881, Lambert Pharmaceutical Company bought the rights to that product and began to market it. The product was very effective at killing germs on soft tissues and worked well as an antiseptic in surgeries.

Did you catch the part about the product being effective at killing germs on soft tissues? What's softer than the tissues inside your mouth? By 1914, dentists realized that the product worked well at killing germs in the mouth, and they concluded that people could gargle with it and, should they swallow it, the product would not kill them. The product was then sold as mouthwash as well as a surgery antiseptic.

My guess is that you have used this product to get rid of bad breath – Lambert came up with the term "halitosis" to mean bad breath. You may not have realized you were gargling with a product used in surgeries, the product Joseph Lawrence named after Joseph Lister . . . **Listerine.**

29: Child-Stay-Away Spray

Sanitize?

When he was busy, my dad hung a circular picture of me and my sister with a line through the picture. Just in case we couldn't figure out the symbolism, it said "No kids beyond this point at this time."

Sometimes in their lives parents just don't have time for kids. They have work to do. Many young adults want to go to college and get their degree before they have kids. These people have no time or money for kids and have no interest in having kids. For these people, wouldn't it be nice if there was a spray or lotion that would make sure that a woman could put on to make sure she would not become a mother?

At one time there was such a spray – or so people thought. In the early 1900s there were no truth-in-advertising laws because people believed "buyer-beware" - if you bought it you did so at your own risk. People relied on their friends and neighbors, not necessarily scientists, for the truth. Although it may sound silly to us, people thought that by having women spraying this product on themselves, the women could keep from becoming mothers. To promote this belief, this product was even marketed to parents assuring them that if women sprayed themselves with it, they would not have kids. In 1933, though, researchers began to question the claims, and they discovered that it worked only about half of the time. By 1960, the product completely dropped such claims. Luckily, for the manufacturer, the product had another use – and this one it was proven very effective at doing.

The spray may have been a flop at keeping kids away, but it was remarkably effective at killing germs. The product had originally been created in 1889 by Gustav Raupenstrauch to protect people from the German Flu. When Covid-19 became common in 2020, people worldwide turned to this germ killer. Today, it comes in aerosol cans and in bottles. Although we can laugh at women spraying it on themselves, we can't deny it is one of the most effective cleaning products around. In fact, your family probably has some of it at home . . . **Lysol.**

30: The Ruined Science Experiment

Where did the bacteria go?

After we eat, I am always careful to put the uneaten food back in the refrigerator. I make sure to seal it thoroughly so that it stays fresh. Despite my best efforts, though, sometimes mold grows on it. For instance, a couple of weeks ago I put some uneaten Pizza Puffs into the refrigerator. They got shoved to the back and forgotten about. When I saw them yesterday, their tan texture had been replaced by a blue-green coating; they had white-spider-like growths and even some gray spots. Needless to say, I did not eat them. It just goes to show you that no matter how careful you are, if you leave food in the refrigerator for too long, mold will likely start to grow.

Alexander Fleming was a researcher who was studying bacteria – Staphylococcus, if you must know – in a petri dish. Scientists try to be careful to make sure their experiments are not contaminated, but somehow mold started to grow in the petri dish. Alexander had been on vacation for two weeks, and he had left the lab unattended during that time. Now that he had returned, he found that the mold was taking over. Not only was the mold growing, but it had also killed the bacteria he was trying to study! His experiment was ruined!

Alexander had failed. He was not going to be able to grow Staph. Alexander didn't focus on the negative side, however. He realized he had made a great discovery - Because of this accident, Alexander learned that some molds could kill bacteria. He realized that when a person is sick with a bacterium, if the person takes some mold the person may get better. This was a major scientific conclusion, and inspired Alexander to investigate different types of mold and their effects on bacteria. Because of this discovery, antibiotics became a field of study. The good mold that Alexander accidently grew, the mold that killed the Staph bacteria, was given a name. It is one of the oldest antibiotics but also still one of the most common . . . *Penicillin.*

31: The Healing Sludge

What's that?

Vaseline. To heal minor skin scraps

Times change, and as time changes, jobs that used to be common disappear. For instance, when the automobile became common, most people who worked building buggies no longer had a job. More recently, people who used to write for the newspaper were displaced because people turned to the Internet. People have to be adaptable.

Robert Chesebrough was a man who had lost his job. Robert was a 22-year-old chemist who studied whales to better understand how to obtain kerosene oil. When oil was discovered in Pennsylvania, people no longer had to rely on kerosene for their lamps or to heat their homes. The company had no use for Robert.

Robert could have given up, but he was curious about this discovery of oil and wondered if there might be an opportunity for a chemist in the new industry. He traveled to Pennsylvania and met the oil rig workers. They showed him around. Robert saw that in the pumping of oil there was some black sludge left behind. The workers cussed the sludge, saying that it built up and ruined their machines, but Robert couldn't help noticing and being fascinated when he saw a couple of the workers placed that sludge on their wounds.

Most people would have thought this sludge-applied-to wounds was just a little quirky and let it go – but not Robert. Robert realized that there might be a chemical reaction between the oil and the wound. In other words, that black sludge on the rod might be a medicine. Curious about the sludge, Robert took some with him to his lab in Brooklyn to study it.

Robert was able to separate the chemicals found in the sludge. He noticed that petroleum jelly was what caused the sludge to be beneficial. After a few experiments, he was able to consistently separate the petroleum jelly from the rest of the rod wax. As he experimented, he found that not only did petroleum jelly work like a lubricant for the oil rigs, but it also worked as a lubricant on other machines. Also, the petroleum jelly had moisturizing qualities as well as healing qualities. In short, he realized that what the oil workers were discarding as trash was very valuable treasure.

He patented the jelly in 1865 and opened a factory that made the jelly in 1870. The product he discovered was petroleum jelly, but Robert didn't think that name would sell any products, so he marked it as "oil water medicine", using the German word for water "vasser" and the Greek word for oil "ileon" but spelling it "ine" to make it sound like medicine. The product still has its original name . . . **Vaseline.**

32: The X-Factor

Have you ever started out to do one thing, but, along the way, get distracted and begin to focus on something else? Most of us have extremely limited attention spans and a great sense of curiosity, so we are constantly starting one thing and then moving on to something else.

Wilhelm Rontgen, a German scientist, began a typical day in his laboratory in Wurzburg, Germany, on November 8, 1895. He was in the process of trying to create a lightbulb by using cathode-ray tubes. On this day, he noticed a mysterious glow coming from a chemically coated screen across the room. He tried to block the rays the screen emitted, but most of the things he put in front of them did not phase the ray. He saw that the cathode tube was sending out not only light but also invisible rays that could penetrate solids.

Rontgen realized he might have found a new type of radiation. He didn't know what the rays were, so he simply called them "x" for "unknown". What he did know was that he could see his bones when he put his hands in front of the glow as if his skin wasn't even there.

Rontgen was so excited about his discovery that he shared it with his wife. He even used the rays to take a picture of her hand. One could clearly see her bones and the wedding ring she wore. The picture created a lot of excitement for the project; Rontgen didn't patent it, though, claiming everyone should have access to the technology. Today, the technology is used in a wide variety of ways. The most common way is by doctors to determine if a bone is broken. Those mysterious rays are understood now, but we still call the pictures what Rongen did . . . *x-rays.*

Chapter Four:
Technology and Electronics

"The digital camera is a great invention
because it allows us to reminisce. Instantly."
~ Demetri Martin

33: He Wanted to Map the Stars

I like to build things with Lego blocks. Sometimes, though, once I have it together, I am afraid to take it apart because I am worried that I won't remember how it went together. I found a way to overcome that worry. I have my dad use the digital camera on his phone and photograph me removing the pieces; this way, I can play it backwards and see exactly where everything went.

I would claim that as an original idea, but it's not. Eugene Lally, an employee of the Jet Propulsion Laboratory came up with that concept in 1961. Eugene was working on two projects for his employer; he wanted to create artificial gravity and he wanted a camera – he called it a photosensor - to capture digital images. His goal was to take pictures of the planets and the stars so the astronauts would have a record of exactly where they had been. These pictures were to help guide the astronauts in determining where they were and to help them get back home.

Lally had come up with the concept, but it was over a decade later before someone was able to invent such a camera. In 1975 Steven Sasson, an Eastman Kodak engineer, invented the digital camera Lally envisioned. The test model was a snapper, that is, it took still shots instead of movies. Although Lally envisioned the camera for space travel, Kodak saw its appeal to the everyday person. Although it saw the appeal, Kodak management was not thrilled with the invention. You see, being digital, the camera required no film. Kodak was in the business of selling and developing film; Kodak saw the new filmless camera as a threat to its existence. And therefore, did not pursue it.

Kodak may have been first to develop the filmless camera, but other companies were also trying to fulfill Lally's vision. Fairchild, Konica, and Sony all came up with filmless cameras as early as 1976. In 1981, Sony introduced the Magnetic Video Camera, the Mavica, a filmless camera that became widely accepted. These filmless cameras still exist today, for both snapshots and for movies, but many people are now beginning to rely on their phones to take their photographs and movies. People don't call them filmless cameras today; you have likely heard them called . . . ***digital cameras.***

34: Bubble, Bubble; The Ink's in Trouble

I like to be prepared. I always carry a pen and a piece of paper with me in case I remember something I was supposed to do, get an idea of something I would like to do, or I am told something I may otherwise forget. I even have pen and paper on my bedside table at night, just in case I wake up with a great idea.

Ichiro Endo also liked to be prepared. He kept a pen on him at all times too. One August day in 1957, he was soldering at a Canon factory in Japan. Not minding what he was doing, he set the hot soldering iron next to his pen; a few seconds later the heat from the soldering iron caused ink to leak – more like to bubble and spit - from the pen.

Ichiro understood the science behind what had happened. Heat had caused the ink to expand. When the ink expanded, it had nowhere to go, so it found the weakest point in the pen and spurted out from it until the pressure was relieved. This observation inspired him, and he made the Canon Bubble Jet Printer a few days after that. The Bubble Jet relied on thermal inkjet technology. The cost of the printer and maintaining it were low, so it became a household device. Today, there are several brand names out there, and you may not have used a Canon Bubble Jet, but you have likely used an . . . *inkjet printer.*

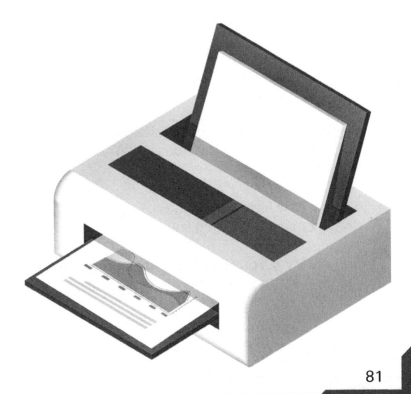

35: "Don't Put All of
Your Eggs in One Basket"

A few days ago, my sister was humming a tune as she did her chores around the house. "Where did you learn that?" my mom asked.

"It's a new song on the radio."
My mom sang the next line with her.

My sister stared in amazement. "How did YOU know it, mom? You don't even listen to the radio."

My mom explained that it was an old song that an artist who was popular today had redone. That's how it is with inventions too. Sometimes we want to give credit to someone for inventing something because they are the ones who did it in our eyes, but other people believe that the credit should be placed elsewhere. For instance, if you were to ask who invented the network of interconnected computers we have today you are likely to get a wide range of answers. Some people would say Leonard Kleinrock, and other people would say J.C.R. Licklider; in the 1960s, both came up with the vision of computers being interconnected. The United States was engaged with Russia in the Cold War, and scientists in the United States were worried that if Russia destroyed a super-computer with all the government's secrets, it could cripple the United States. They both envisioned a network of computers that interacted with one another. Because all the computers were intertwined should one of the computers be destroyed, the rest would keep running. It was a strategy built around "don't put all of your eggs in one basket."

Vinton Cerf and Bob Kahn were the programmers who turned the idea into reality. They invented a code - TCP/IP (Transmission Control Protocol/Internet Protocol), a suite of communication protocols used to interconnect network devices on the Internet. This is the figurative handshake that links two computers together.

Using Internet cables and Bluetooth, your computer can communicate with computers around the world – as well as with the person next door. Today, electronic-mail (email) and the World Wide Web (www) make up the biggest chunks of these interconnected computers, but that may not be what constitutes the network tomorrow.

You may not have realized it, but no single person put this network of computers together. Likewise, no single person has total control over this network of interconnected computers, this network we know as . . . *the Internet.*

36: It was Intended to be a Gift, Not a New Invention

There are a lot of ways to show our friends that they are special. One way is by spending time with them. Another is to hug them. Still another is by giving them small gifts. Jack Kelley was the gift-giving kind of friend.

Jack Kelley was a friend of Douglas Engelbart. Not only were they friends, but they were also co-workers at the Herman Miller furniture store. Doug, a veteran of World War II, tinkered with inventions, and in the early 1960s, he and his friend Bill English had developed a device that would move the cursor on the computer screen so that a keyboard was not needed. Doug called his invention the "mouse" because it was short, stubby, and had a tail that attached to the computer. Doug's device consisted of a button on a wood block with pizza-cutter-like wheels underneath it. Jack heard that Doug was going to show off the invention at an exhibit called "The Mother of all Demos" in 1968.

To encourage his friend, Jack made a gift - Jack created a pad for the mouse. The pad ensured that the mouse rolled smoothly by creating friction for its wheels. Also, it reminded the user to stay within its boundaries and enabled the movements of the mouse to be more precise. The pad's fabric also provided a wrist rest, as well as added some color and pizazz to draw the eyes of those who passed. The pad was meant as a gift for his friend; it was not intended to be an invention to complement his friend's invention.

Doug took both the mouse and the pad to the exhibit. At a time when people were used to writing commands of code, the mouse seemed too simplistic. Although the mouse flopped in 1968, technicians saw potential for it as computers got less complicated and gradually became acquired by people not skilled in extensive programming. The technicians also reworked the mouse replacing the wheels with a trackball.

In 1988, Apple sold its Macintosh with a mouse. Jack's gift was also part of Apple's package; a pad for the mouse to operate. Jack had not intended to invent anything, but he had invented something extremely useful to complement what Doug had invented. Jack's invention led to a fad – people enjoyed personalizing the pad on which they kept their mouse. Jack thought of it as just a fabric covering and didn't even realize it was an invention, let alone something that needed to be named, but you have likely heard a name for his invention; we call it . . . *the mousepad.*

37: The Magic Button

Wouldn't it be nice if you could push a button and all your chores were done? People have wished for that kind of device for years.

Nikola Tesla, a famous inventor at the turn of the twentieth century, created such a product – but he didn't realize it. Instead, Nikola believed he had created the driverless ship. To prove this, in 1898 he put a toy boat in a giant pool at Madison Square Garden in New York City. The boat had a small antenna that could pick up radio waves he sent from the control box he held in his hand. The signals shifted different electrical contacts, causing the boat's rudder and propeller to move. The U.S. Navy was not impressed. (However, in World War I, the Germans used this technology to send unmanned submarines ramming into Allied boats.)

In the 1950s, Eugene McDonald, president of Zenith in the United States, had a pet peeve – he hated commercials on his television. He wanted his engineers to find a way to either mute the commercial or to let him flip from channel to channel without getting out of his chair. At first, they came up with the Lazy Bone, a device that allowed people sitting in their chairs to change the channels and mute the television by pushing buttons on a hand-held box– but the Lazy Bone was attached to the television by wire, and many people tripped over the wire. Next, they tried a remote control that worked based on light; if the remote control was pointed at the sensor, the television followed the command given. This idea did not work well either, because sunlight would also hit those sensors, causing chaos. Finally, they applied Tesla's concept of radio waves.

Today people use Tesla's technology for opening and closing their garage doors, turning on and off lights, and, of course, adjusting settings on the television. The name of the device reflects the fact that one does not have to be present to make the item work; that is, one can work it remotely. Therefore, we call Tesla's invention . . . **the remote.**

38: Dust with Brains

Have you ever stood by a window and watched dust dance in the sunlight? Isn't it amazing that all those particles are in the air but that we seldom pay attention to them? Dust is incredibly tiny and minute. Our homes are full of dust. (Yes, mom, even our house, even though I know you and dad work hard to keep it clean.) Normally, dust comes from dead skin cells, fabrics, and outside substances such as pollen and dirt.

Dust can also be created by sawing or smashing something. For instance, one day in 2003 Jamie Link, a doctoral student at the University of California, was working on a silicon chip in a lab when the chip suddenly exploded. Dust went everywhere – some of it though was not dust, it was actually pieces of the chip. To her amazement, the sensors, such as a motion detector, moisture detector, and light detector - continued to work. These little sensors were dust-sized, but they still gave off their signal and they could still be controlled by radio signals from someone far away. Until this moment, no one had thought of using the dust-sized pieces outside of the chip.

People began to see instant uses for her invention. The military realized it would be excellent for spying on enemies. Doctors realized they could have a patient swallow a little speck and then see inside the patient's body. Construction workers realized that if these sensors were embedded in pavement, the sensors could assist driverless cars. When Jamie created these sensors, it was by accident, but today they are created on purpose. This dust certainly is intelligent; it's no wonder she decided to call it . . . ***smart dust.***

39: The Talking Wire

Hello!

Do you have a passion for helping? Some people really like to help other people. By making other people feel better, they feel better about themselves. Their passion creates great enthusiasm, and they throw themselves wholeheartedly into the project, not worrying about the cost of time or resources.

Alexander Graham Bell had such a passion; his passion was for deaf people. (Both his mother and his wife were deaf.) Because of this interest, he studied sound. He was interested in how sound traveled and how sound could be recorded. Bell had found others who shared his passion, and they helped to fund his experiments. Bell had also met Thomas Watson, an electrician; Bell was an idea-person and Watson was a hands-on person who could bring Bell's ideas to reality.

Beginning in 1874, Bell and Watson officially worked on a machine that could transmit several telegraphs at once using different frequency levels – this experiment helped to fund Bell's lab. On the side, though, they worked on a machine that they were truly passionate about, one that did more than just pay the bills - they were working on a machine that would carry the human voice over a wire.

One day – March 10, 1876 to be exact - as they tinkered, Bell suddenly heard Watson from across the room – what he heard, though, was coming from the wire. Bell enthusiastically called, "Mister Watson, come here. I want to see you." The wire not only carried sound from Watson; it carried sound to Watson. Watson heard the talking wire – he had received the first phone call.

Bell began Bell Labs in 1877, a company that placed phones in businesses and installed wires to connect them. Bell had ideas about his invention and his company that seem foreign to us today. Bell thought that the proper way to greet someone when answering the phone was to say, "Ahoy", the customary greeting sailors give to each other. (Thomas Edison was the one who proposed using the greeting "Hello.") Bell also believed that only businesses would be interested in buying his products; he did not think that people in their residences had enough to say to each other to justify having a phone – soon, though, his product was in both businesses and residences.

Bell would likely be amazed if he could see what his invention had become. His invention no longer depends on wires going from one place to another; people can call on it at any time from almost anywhere. His invention is used for much more than calling; it is used to take pictures, to check the temperature, to play music, to compute, to write on as if it were a date book, and so much more. Although it has changed a lot, we still call the invention by what he called it, . . . **the telephone.**

40: Hidden Talents

Can you water ski?

That question may never have crossed your mind until now. Unless you live by a big lake where motorboats are plentiful, you have probably never had the opportunity to try. Because you have never tried it, you probably assume that you can't, but, once you actually try it, you may find that you can. (By the way, I can water ski. It's a lot of fun.)

Cell phones work much the same way. We don't even think about the possibility of them doing certain things, and, because we have never asked if it can be done, we simply assume that it cannot be done. Cell phones, like many technological devices, can do much more than they are actually programmed to do. In 1984, Friedhelm Hillebrand and Bernard Ghillebaert developed a short message service (SMS) that would allow them to send brief messages back and forth on their cell phones so they could better manage networks. This was something the phone could do but that the average person was not supposed to be aware that it could do.

Secrets are hard to keep, though, and the general public found out what the phone could do. Friedhelm and Bernard – call them Fred and Barney if you are their close friend – had intended to create a way of keeping in touch with each, but instead they developed a whole new function for the cell phone. The first time the system was used for nonbusiness was December 3, 1992, when Richard Jarvis wished Neil Papworth, "Merry Christmas." When you and I write things such as "lol" which stands for "lots of laughs" and "idk" which stands for "I don't know" we are using their short message service. You may or may not have heard it called SMS, but you have likely heard of . . . *texting.*

Chapter Five:
Accidental Inventions in the Kitchen

"Everything happens in the kitchen.
Life happens in the kitchen."
~ *Andrew Zimmern*

41: A Sewing Kit Led to a Bright Idea

Have you ever been in a crisis and heard something like, "Quick, get me something to plug this hole"? When you heard it, you likely looked around the room and then grabbed the first workable object.

That is exactly what William Murdock did too. William was in his workshop in 1792 (or 1794, the record is not clear). He had been experimenting with gas and he had a gas flame coming out of a pipe in his lab, and, since it was time to quit, he wanted to snuff it out. He glanced around the room, looking for something that could snuff out the flame. The first workable object that he saw was his wife's sewing thimble, so he thrust it over the light. Not able to receive any oxygen to keep burning, the flame went out.

William, though, could still smell gas. To see if the pipe was leaking gas, William lit a match by the thimble. With the gas lit, he could clearly see it seeping through the little holes in the thimble. That was a surprise! What surprised him the most, though, was that the flame burning through the holes was much more intense than the flame had been when it was burning as a whole at the end of the pipe.

In the 1800s gas lights lined the public streets. Unintentionally, William had just discovered how to make them burn brighter without using more gas. Gas lamps are sometimes used still today in some towns as streetlamps and on lawns for decoration; William's invention also transferred to burners on the gas stove. William didn't call his accidental invention a "thimble for gas pipes", he believed the flames coming from it looked like thorns or cockspurs, so he called it . . . ***the cockspur gas burner.***

42: How a Gun Cleaner Became a Bottle Opener

Have you ever thrown a rock into a lake and watched as the rock creates a ripple which then creates a ripple that then creates another ripple? It's a beautiful sight.

Many times, life's events ripple like that. When you do one thing, it causes something to happen that then causes something else to happen. Prior to the late 1600s, every bottle was uniquely created by a glass blower, and no two bottles were exactly alike. When people learned how to pour glass into molds to make bottles, though, all the bottles were exactly the same – this meant they stacked and shipped nicely. Manufacturers could choose what they wanted their bottles to look like and then create the desired mold – wine makers chose to have their

bottles be tall and slender, have straight sides, and contain cylinder necks. This design allowed them to be laid on their side for easy storage and shipment.

This, though, created a ripple. If the bottles were on their sides, they had to be sealed so they could not leak. Wine manufacturers realized that by compressing cork and then forcing it into the neck of the bottle, they could create a very tight seal. Problem solved!

However, this in turn created another ripple. The corks were sealed so tightly, they were hard to remove. Just as you and I do today when we get a package that is well wrapped, we use whatever we can get our hands on – scissors, pocket-knives, someone's fingernails – to try to open it. When people got hold of these corked bottles that were almost impossible to open, someone had the idea of using a gun-worm to open it. (A gun worm was a device people inserted into guns to remove a stuck bullet.) The first record of the gun worm being used to remove a cork is from 1681. Someone believed if it could unplug a gun, it could unplug a bottle!

People called the repurposing of the gun worm a new invention, and merchants began to market it as the "bottlescrew." In 1720 it took on a new name . . . *the corkscrew.*

43: From 68 to 840 Degrees Fahrenheit in a Single Second

On one of those hot, hot summer days have you ever gone into a cold, cold place? One day my friends and I received a tour of a fast-food establishment. The guide let us walk through the hot, hot grill area and then, seconds later, took us into the large walk-in refrigerator, and then into the walk-in freezer. My body had barely adjusted to the heat of the grill, and it was not happy at all about the freezing temperatures.

Cookware is much the same way. When it goes from sitting on a cabinet at room temperature to a kitchen oven that is 400 degrees or hotter in the next second, it can crack because of the extreme temperature difference. Fortunately, our dishes today are made of materials that do not crack under sudden temperature changes. We have people like S. Donald Stookey to thank for that.

S. Donald Stookey was working at Corning Research and Development in 1953. He was testing glass and thought he had put the glass into an oven of 600 degrees; he came to find out, it was 900 degrees. The substance, though, hadn't cracked as would be expected; it had just turned a milky white. Thinking the glassware was trash because he had overheated it, he took tongs to remove it. As he pulled milky, hot glassware out of the furnace, he accidently dropped it – and it didn't shatter.

He realized then that he had invented a white glass-ceramic capable of withstanding sudden temperature changes. He called the invention Pyroceram. The Corning company found a lot of uses for the material, including making missile nose cones and pieces of the space shuttle. You have likely seen his milky white temperature-resistant material in the kitchen of your house too; it is used to manufacture a lot of cookware. We don't call the dishes made from it Pyroceram, though, we call them . . . ***Corningware - now known as Pyrex.***

44: The Lesser and the Grater

Have you ever gotten frustrated with an object? For instance, have you been tempted to shake your computer or throw an alarm clock?

If you have, you understand how Lorraine Lee, a Canadian homemaker, was feeling when she tried to grate oranges for an Armenian orange cake one day in 1994. Her grater was simply not getting the job done. Frustrated, she reached into a sack of tools her husband had left on the counter from a trip to their hardware store, Lee Valley Tools. She took the new wood grater, a microplane rasp from the sack, sneered an evil sneer of revenge, and then ran the grater across the orange, releasing all her anger and frustrations.

The orange pieces were both beautiful and tasty. She was so impressed with the shards of zest that the microplane created that

she listed it as a kitchen tool in their next hardware catalog instead of a woodworking tool. She had just created the microplane grater.

The microplane rasp itself was a fairly new invention. Grace Manufacturing, a company in Arkansas that used to make dot-matrix printers, was on the verge of going out of business since most dot matrix printers had become replaced with inkjet and laser printer technology. Its owner, Mark Grace, realized that the company made a lot of sharp pieces – he had the Band-Aid wrappers to prove it, and he wondered if there was a market for a knife-like product.

He realized his sharp product would be different from others in the industry. The sharp holes his company put in metal were not smelted; they were burned into the metal by a chemical. This burning resulted in extremely smooth edges; therefore, the final product would not tear or shred like most competitors' products did.

The company decided to manufacture a microplane, a foot-long tool with razor-like incisions, that could be used to sand boards. Lorrainne's husband had brought one home that day to do exactly that. (A moral to the story: When you get married, always put away anything you value; if your spouse finds it laying around, no telling what they will use it for.)

The microplane had not sold exceptionally well as a wood cutter, but as a fruit and vegetable cutter, sales began to soar. When the microplane's kitchen prowess was featured in a *New York Times* article and then on the *QVC* television show, sales flourished. Today most modern kitchens consider it a necessity to have a . . . *Microplane Grater.*

45: The Melted Granola Bar

Popcorn!

Have you ever gone outside and simply marveled at nature? You may see a squirrel running here, then running there, and then walking on a telephone line like a trapeze artist. You may hear birds sing. Perhaps you can even see ants gathering food as they march in unison.

Percy Lebaron Spencer loved nature; in particular, he loved squirrels. Percy grew up in Maine, and he could see squirrels every day. He believed squirrels had the right idea for good health – to snack on nuts and grains. Therefore, everyday Percy took a granola bar of nuts and grains to work in his pocket for a snack.

Percy was a researcher for the U.S. military. One day in 1945 when he had finished testing a military-grade magnetron, a radar device which used microwaves, he went to take his granola bar from his pocket – and he found that it had melted. Melted? Chocolate bars are known to melt in pockets from one's body heat, but granola bars don't melt from body heat. He realized that it would have taken intense heat to have melted that granola bar in his pocket. Where did this intense heat come from? Obviously, the magnetron. He also realized that the melting was accomplished within just a few seconds.

Being a curious fellow, he put an egg in the magnetron and then turned it on. The egg literally exploded in his face seconds later. (Research can be messy; this researcher literally had egg on his face.) The next day, he put corn kernels in the magnetron, and he came out with popcorn – a snack that he shared with his coworkers.

Today, we don't call that cooking device the magnetron, but we still use it to cook popcorn and other foods. Whereas most workplaces did not have a magnetron-like device in the 1940s, today, almost all do as a courtesy to their employees – and most homes have one as well. The magnetron is better known as . . . *the microwave oven.*

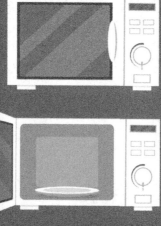

46: They Burned His Bread Once Too Often

When you go to a restaurant, how do you know you got a good meal? Do you look at the presentation of the food, making sure it is neatly placed on the plate? Do you ponder the taste of the food? Do you consider if the order took a long time to get ready? Do you look at the cost of the food compared to the amount of food you got? Most people have one or two things from this list they focus on.

Charles Strite focused on speed and quality. Charles loved toast, and toast was popular in society in 1919. Charles did not set out to invent anything; he just wanted to figure out how to get a consistently good piece of toast - something he was not able to do.

Alan MacMasters, a Scottish inventor, had invented the electric toaster between 1883 and 1893, and so by 1919 people no

longer made toast by hand-flipping the bread on the grill. The electric toaster allowed toast to be mass produced, and it was a common breakfast staple. Unfortunately, Alan's invention only toasted on one side of the bread and then the bread had to be turned over and run through the machine again. Alan's invention had a second flaw as well; someone had to pull the toast out of the toaster, and, in busy restaurants, kitchen staff was often too busy to do so – this resulted in a lot of burnt toast.

One day, Charles had had enough. Day after day in the company cafeteria he had gotten burnt toast. Charles didn't bother talking to the manager; he could see how overworked the employees were and he knew what the problem was. Charles came up with a machine, the Toastmaster, that could toast on both sides of the bread simultaneously. His invention improved the toaster in a second way as well - it had a timer that, once the time was reached, would release a spring which would turn off the heating element and pop the toast up.

Charles formed Waters Genter Company and began to sell the Toastmaster to restaurants. Soon, people in the restaurants wanted a version of the Toastmaster that they could use at home, and, beginning in 1926, Charles met the need. The original Toastmaster only had one setting - Charles has assumed everyone liked the same degree of toastiness as he did, but that was not the case. Having received numerous complaints that the toast was too raw or too burnt, he added an adjustable timer so people could brown the bread to suit their personal preference.

Charles called his invention the Toastmaster, and the Toastmaster is still available today. You may not have heard of the Toastmaster, for that has become a brand name, but you likely have heard of . . . *the pop-up toaster.*

47: Trouble on the Horizon

Have you ever seen black storm clouds in the distance, making their way toward you? I used to live in Kansas, and tornados can come up very quickly in Kansas. If you see dark clouds in the distance, you can rest assured that the wind that is a gentle breeze at the moment will soon be high gusts removing anything in their way. The sky that appears so blue over you right now will soon be replaced with dark purple skies and black clouds – even though it is in the middle of the afternoon – stretching as far as one can see. The clouds in the distance are a warning to prepare.

Harry Brearley saw trouble on the horizon. It was 1913 in England and a clash with the Germans appeared likely. Harry knew to prepare for the storm, and so he was trying to make gun barrels that would not rust from the weather and would not wear down from bullets exiting them. To make the barrels, he combined different metals to steel. His efforts were not getting far until one day when he combined chromium to steel. When he tried to clean the resulting product, he found that it resisted the cleaner.

It not only resisted the cleaner, but it also resisted rust. He called his accidental invention "rustless steel." The war did come, and from 1914-1918 the war halted his further experimentation.

After the war, Harry went back to experimenting. He saw a second use for his new metal besides gun barrels – cooking utensils. Many knives, pots, and pans rusted fast, and rust was not healthy to digest. Harry believed kitchen utensils could be made from his "rustless steel." Ernest Stuart, a cutlery manufacturer, changed the name of the invention from "rustless steel" and, overtime, Ernest's name became the accepted term. You may never have heard the term "rustless steel" but Harry's invention is all around us - in guns, in construction projects, and in kitchens - and you have probably heard Ernest's name for it . . . ***stainless steel.***

48: Keep Thinking

Have you ever brainstormed for an idea, come up with an idea, and then quit thinking? Lots of people do. Researchers believe that the first idea we usually have is fairly traditional, and, if we want to be creative, we really need to keep thinking of a second, third, and fourth idea as well. The first ideas may be good ideas and ones that have been proven to work, but they are not always the best ideas.

Roy Plunkett realized the truth of what the researchers were saying about creativity. On April 6, 1938 Roy Plunkett, a DuPont chemist, was trying to improve the cooling mechanism of the refrigerator and air conditioner. He mixed different chemical combinations and allowed them to sit. Later, when he opened the container, he found a white powdery, waxy, water-repelling, non-stick substance that was resistant to heat.

What could a person do with a non-stick substance that resisted heat? Some people would have thrown it out; it definitely was not refrigerator coolant. Roy and DuPont, though, found many uses for it, and began to market products, such as beauty products, with it in 1946. Even today, it is used in make-up and beauty products. The most common use for it though, was not found until 1954.

In 1954, Marc Gregoire's wife asked Marc to coat her pans with the substance so that food would not stick to her pan. Marc, a French engineer for DuPont, did as she said. Today, most pots and pans are coated with this substance. It took sixteen years to find this use for the product - the first answer was not the best answer, but once this new use was thought of it changed the world. Some ideas take a long, long time to think of! Cooks loved the innovation of non-stick pans. Although Roy called the new polymer he had discovered "polytetrafluoroethylene," most people simply say their pans are covered with . . . **Teflon.**

49: Making Use of Every Scrap

I am concerned about our environment. I try not to waste anything. I believe in being a good steward of what I was given, and I want to leave the earth in good shape for the next generation.

William Hadaway, the man who invented the electric stove on June 30, 1896, had a similar approach to life. He didn't like to waste materials. His boss, General Electric, paid for the materials, and the company didn't like wasted materials either. However, whenever Hadaway made an electric stove, there were waste materials. Hadaway wondered what he could do with these scraps? He began to tinker, and, voila! although he didn't set out with the goal in mind, in 1910 he made a toaster-cooker oven from those waste materials.

His oven was similar to other toasters that were out on the market at the time – the first electric toaster appeared in 1906 - in which people inserted their bread vertically. His toaster-cooker, though, had one major difference – people inserted the bread horizontally. This meant that not only bread could be toasted just like in other toasters, but so could pizza and numerous other products.

The toaster-cooker was more like an electric oven than a toaster, for it had a front door, a wire rack, and a removable baking pan to toast bread. The toaster-cooker was larger than a toaster, but it was much smaller than an electric oven. The toaster-cooker could do many of the same things as the electric oven could do, just on a smaller scale. Toaster-cookers are still around today. The technology has not changed much since 1910, but instead of calling them toaster-cookers, we call them . . . *toaster ovens.*

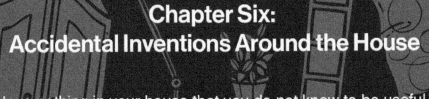

Chapter Six:
Accidental Inventions Around the House

Have nothing in your house that you do not know to be useful,
or believe to be beautiful."
~ *William Morris*

50: Bug Bombs

Have you ever played hide-and-seek on a hot summer day? If you have, you know that it is not just the person who is searching for you that you have to watch out for. You must also be on guard for mosquitoes, horseflies, and other annoying critters that want to suck your blood and otherwise make you miserable.

During World War II, U.S. servicemen found themselves in hostile territory. It wasn't just the enemy troops that they had to be aware of – more people were being killed by bug bites than by bullets. (Not only were the bugs in the Pacific islands annoying, but they also carried malaria.) Knowing his country

was desperate for a solution, Lyle D. Goodhue, an employee in the U.S. Department of Agriculture, reminded his supervisors that he had suggested that insecticide should be sprayed from a can using liquid halogen hydrocarbons, but that his idea had never been tested.

Goodhue found an ally in William N. Sullivan – Sullivan was willing to work with Goodhue to test if being sprayed from a can was an effective way of delivering insecticide. The tests proved to be highly successful, and portable cylinders known as "bug bombs" were developed for the soldiers to use.

After they won the war and returned to civilian life, many former U.S. soldiers searched the Army surplus store for the cans of insecticide. They had pests in their homes, on their porches, and at their barbeques - none of the carried malaria, but they were pests just the same. They recalled that the special can used by the Army enabled the sprayer to target the pest, making using the insecticide highly effective and cost efficient.

As the soldiers sought out these cans, factory owners soon realized that insecticide was just one product that could be delivered by these cans. Hairspray was another. Manufacturers replaced the can's expensive copper knob with a plastic one and began to mass market canned products.

Lyle and William did not invent this special can. The can and the concept of using pressure to remove the can's contents was developed by a Norwegian, Erik Andreas Rotheim, in the 1920s and 1930s. However, Erik had not found anything to put in the can that the public wanted to buy. Lyle and William were the first to find a practical use for it and today, even though it was found to be detrimental to the environment before it was revamped, that special can is still used for hairspray, insecticide, and numerous other products. That special can, which may not seem so special since you see it every day is . . . *the aerosol can.*

51: The Birth of "Pop" Culture

Have you ever had an idea that you thought was great but found that nobody else liked it?

In 1957, Alfred Fielding and Marc Chavannes, two Sealed Air engineers, had an idea of a unique wallpaper. They thought that lining walls with strips of plastic coated with sealed bubbles could be the next big thing in home decorating; they thought that bamboo, which was the latest wall fad among the youth, could be successful, then sealed bubbles could be the next fad. They believed in the idea so much, they created two shower curtains with their bubble strips for the Sealed Air board to see. Their three-dimensional (3-D) textured wallpaper idea was rejected.

They kept brainstorming possible uses for strips of bubbles of sealed air. Their second idea also involved the sealed air bubbles being wall covering, but this time it was not for decorative purposes. They had noticed that their sealed bubbles on plastic strips would allow the sun to come through while providing some insulation from cold outdoor weather, so they tried to appeal to greenhouses to install the strips of bubbles. Sealed Air agreed to let Alfred and Marc market their product to greenhouses, but greenhouse owners were not interested in their product.

The concept of using the strips of bubbles as insulation inspired Alfred and Mac to find a third way to market it. They had noticed that the bubbles on the shower curtain had a bounce; that is, they could hold weight and not break. What if they could use strips of bubbles as insulation in shipping? They received permission from Sealed Air to see if anyone would be interested in using their product in this way.

Fred Bowers, a marketer for IBM, was very interested. Fred had lots of fragile computer parts to ship in 1960, and he realized that the bubbles made a great cushion. Not only were the bubbles effective as a cushioning agent, but the bubbles also weighed almost nothing. Fred, Alfred, and Marc didn't realize one thing – When Fred's customers received their computer parts, they received a bonus – a sheet of bubbles they could pop. Fred's customers loved the product as insulation but also as a toy, and they were inclined to order more products from Fred just to get more bubbles.

Alfred and Mac hadn't intentionally made a shipping product, but their product is still used in shipping today. You have probably even popped a few bubbles from packages yourself from time to time. Those sheets of plastic bubbles, which began as potential wallpaper and then greenhouse insulation still have the name, they were originally given . . . **Bubble Wrap.**

52: The Invisible Sheet

Have you ever been in a restaurant and watched somebody accidentally spill something? What was your reaction? Did you feel embarrassed for them? Did you clap to draw attention to them and embarrass them? Did you rush over with napkins? Did you laugh? Did you nudge your friend, point, and make a snarky comment? Did you pretend that nothing happened? There are lots of potential reactions to an accidental spill.

Jacques Brandenberger, a Swiss, was sitting in a restaurant in 1900 when he saw someone spill a glass of wine. Jacques did none of the above. When Jacques saw the wine spill, his reaction was "I wonder if I could invent a material that would repel liquid instead of absorb it?"

Jacques's curiosity caused him to try to do exactly that. He reasoned that the best thing to do was to spray a waterproof coating onto an already existing fabric. For the next eight years, Jacques tried coating fabrics with different materials. In 1908, he had yet another failure. He took liquid viscose (a cellulose product made from trees), applied it onto a fabric, and found that the resulting fabric was too heavy and that the covering he had created peeled right off.

Wait a minute, he thought. That bioplastic that peeled right off might not work well as a table covering, but it might be able to be used for other things. He shifted gears, now focusing on the bioplastic transparent film. He realized he had created a thin, flexible film that had many potential uses. By 1912, he was manufacturing the product, and during World War I it was being used in the production of gas masks.

Today, his product is used in the food industry to keep food fresh and bacteria-free while allowing potential customers to see the food item. In many cases, petroleum now is often substituted for cellulose when making the product. Jacques gave the product a name that means "transparent cellulose," the name . . . **cellophane.**

53: Being Prepared for a Rainy Day as if Your Life Depended on It

Have you ever been carrying a sheet of homework to school when the clouds started to sprinkle? You knew that the paper would get ruined if it got wet, and you likely did everything possible to keep it dry.

Now, pretend you are in the trenches in World War II. Your life depends on gunpowder, for that keeps the enemy from getting too close. As you know, it rains on battlefronts just like it does on paths to school, and your life literally depends on that ammunition staying dry. The U.S. Army has provided big plastic containers to carry the ammunition, but these plastic containers have overlapping lips that leak; water is able to get between the lips. That leak is going to ruin the ammunition. So, what do you do?

Fortunately for them, in addition to the leaking containers, U.S. soldiers had also been given a three-ply tape. The khaki-colored tape consisted of a fabric mesh with a water-resistant covering and a rubber-based adhesive. The tape was khaki colored, so it blended into the ammunition chest. The tape worked extremely well. It was easy to tear, easy to apply, and stuck where it was placed.

Of course, it didn't rain all of the time, so bored soldiers would play with the tape on sunny days while sitting around the campsite. They found numerous uses for it, including patching holes on their tents, patching holes in their boots, and strapping loads onto jeeps. When the war ended, most of these soldiers returned to civilian life. They loved that water-resistant multi-purpose tape and requested it from the Army surplus stores. To meet the rising demand, a silver-grey version of it was released to the general public. Because it was water-resistant, many soldiers called it, "Duck Tape." John Denoye and Bill Gross, the creators of the tape who worked at Johnson & Johnson, had called it "gun tape," but, when they released the silver-grey version of it to the general public, they acknowledged the soldiers' term and named it . . . ***duct tape.***

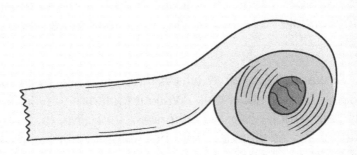

54: This Inventor Talked Hot Air

Have you ever heard your mom say, "You need to dry your hair before you go outside; if you don't, you will catch a cold"? Medical science has found truth to that statement, and therefore people have been drying their hair before going outside for years.

Alexander Godefroy was a male, and like most males in the 1890s, he had short hair. While it took him very little time to dry his hair, it took his wife Catherine a long time to dry her hair. He often watched her do what the ladies of his era did – they dried their hair with the vacuum cleaner.

Now before you get the wrong idea, remember that vacuums suck air up hoses. At the other end of the vacuum is the motor, where the sucked air is able to escape after all of the dirt has been left behind in the vacuum's filter. Women used to turn the vacuum on, and then let that warm air which was being put out by the vacuum blow on their hair.

Godefroy, who owned a hair salon in France, had an idea. Why not create a machine similar to the vacuum that could blow warm air over a person's head? He created such a machine in 1890. He had women put on a bonnet that would receive hot air through a pipe; the hot air originated at a nearby gas stove. His bonnet had holes on the inside so that the warm air could flow freely. His beauty parlor was a success. He kept the idea to himself for a while, but, in 1920, he realized the financial potential his invention had, and he began to sell his invention of piping and domes to other beauty parlors.

These hot air domes are still used in many beauty parlors around the world today. Between wanting to help the world and to make some money off the hair-drying fad, other people began to build on Godefroy's idea. The first blow dryer was created in 1911; it looked like a reverse vacuum, and – for all intents and purposes, it was - instead of sucking air up, it breathed hot air on the female until her hair was dry.

The vacuum cleaner was meant to be an object that picked up dirt, not inspire other inventions. However, clever people noticed other uses for the vacuum and people like Godefroy noticed what these clever people did and made a fortune off it. Today, we don't always think of its roots, but it is likely you have used Godefroy's invention to dry your hair. It has three names in popular culture – the blow dryer, the hairdryer, or as Godefroy called it . . . *the hair dryer.*

55: The Good Neighbor

Are you the kind of person who helps someone when they have a need? I hope you are; I try to be.

Ed Lowe tried to be a good neighbor. Ed was in the business of selling ice, coal, sand, sawdust, and granulated kiln-dried clay. (The clay was used to put on oil spills, and, in those days, cars slowly leaking oil was a common problem.) One day in 1947, Ed's neighbor asked for some sand for her kitty's litter box. She had been using ashes and found that too messy; her cat was putting sooty paw prints throughout the house. Ed was

glad to help and was going to give her a bag of sand, but, it was cold outside, and Ed found that his packages of sand were frozen. Frustrated by still wanting to help her, Ed gave her some of the granulated kiln-dried clay to try.

When he saw his neighbor next, he asked her how it was going with the cat and the granulated clay. She said the granulated clay did a great job of keeping odor down; keeping odors down was something ashes, torn newspaper, or dirt – the three common things people used in litter boxes – were not able to do. His neighbor spread the word about the success she had with the clay pellets, and soon Ed had many orders for the granulated kiln-dried clay. He had so many order that, in 1953, he decided to start marketing the product to pet stores as well as his neighbors. Although cats had lived outdoors – utilizing flowerbeds and backyards to deposit their poop, housecats had become very common in the 1940s, and there was a great need for his product. The name he gave the product clearly defined the contents - Kitty Litter. In 1954, he changed the product's name to what you know it as . . . ***Tidy Cat brand of kitty litter.***

Do you have allergies? Some people are allergic to mold, hay, fur, and even certain foods. If you have allergies, your body tends to sneeze or otherwise react when it comes in contact with the item it cannot tolerate.

Ernst Mahler, the head of research at Kimberly-Clark, had hay fever. Pollen made his eyes water and his nose run. Not wanting to wipe his nose on his shirt – he was the head of research and that would have been undignified, he grabbed

a package of paper tissues that the company made that were designed for removing cold crème. As he went around the factory, he would discretely – if there is such a thing – blow his nose and then throw away the tissue.

People in marketing saw that he was using the tissue as a disposable handkerchief. They realized that if he could do it, so could other people, so they started to market the product as "the handkerchief you can throw away." Sales of the product doubled, and soon the brand name and the term "facial tissue" were interchangeable. The product had begun in 1924 as cold crème wipes but, after Mahler's sneezing fit in 1929, became even more known as a disposable handkerchief; today, when you need to blow your nose you are likely to reach for . . . *a Kleenex.*

Sometimes there is a greater demand for things than there are for things to go around. For instance, if four of my friends and I walk into the house to ask mom for a chocolate chip cookie each and there are only two chocolate chip cookies, it would seem that we are either going to have to share or that two people will be doing without any cookie. That was all the solutions my friends and I could think of, but my mom had a third option: Perhaps something could substitute for a chocolate-chip cookie, such as some snickerdoodle cookies – and she had plenty of those to go around!

Leo Baekeland was a Belgium-American chemist who thought like my mom. He knew there was a great demand for a secretion by a particular beetle – people wanted to use it as a varnish. There were very few beetles and each beetle produced a minute amount, so what secretion was available was very expensive. Leo believed he could create the same chemical in his lab that the beetle created, and he set about to do it.

In 1907, Leo tried lots of combinations in his Yonkers, New York lab, but none worked. One combination he created, though, appealed to him – it was moldable, durable and heat resistant, but it didn't conduct electricity; these traits made it perfect for kitchenware, telephones, and electronics. Leo did not succeed in finding a chemical shellac, but what he found changed our daily life much, much more.

The scientific name for Leo's creation is polyoxybenzylmethylenglycolanhydride. Leo, who had a bit of an ego, named the product after himself, calling it Bakelite. Bakelite was the first generation of a substance you likely have within your reach . . . *plastic.*

58: They Had it for a Song

Do you like to sing? I do too. I usually tab the pages of my music book so that I can jump readily from one song to another without having to spend time flipping through the book.

Art Fry, a 3M employee, had the same strategy. Art liked to sing in his church choir and, to make going from song to song easy, he liked to mark the hymnal's pages. Unfortunately, the papers he used as bookmarks were prone to fall out.

Art was one of those people who respected books. Folding the page down – "dog ear" style – was not an acceptable solution. Neither was using large items like paper clips, for they often left rust spots and almost always left indentations on the

page. Suddenly he remembered that his friend at 3M, Spencer Silver, had invented a portable bulletin board, a piece of paper that could be placed on the wall and then removed without leaving any residue. He wondered if that same piece of paper could be shrunk to bookmark size and then placed in his hymnal. Once he was done singing, he could remove the paper and not leave any trace of it in the hymnbook.

Spencer was delighted with Art's idea of a sticky note. Spencer had created the glue that would not stick by accident in 1968; he was trying to create a new super glue. He was fascinated with his failure, though, and believed there must be a use for it. Building on Art's idea, in 1977, 3M released Press and Peel, sheets of paper that had the glue on them that could be pressed against anything and then peeled.

Press and Peel papers were distributed to four cities; few sold. The marketing department said to give up, but a manager wanted to give the product one more chance. 3M then gave away the product to everyone in Boise, Idaho; the results were amazing - 90% of the people and businesses that received the product for free reordered in the near future – they loved it. The product's name soon changed from "Press and Peel" to the name you know the product by today . . . **Post-It Notes.**

59: The Protective Father

Have you ever seen how protective mothers are over their baby – especially the first one. They worry that one little mistake can cause a major injury. They love their child, and they want the best for it. They believe the child is delicate and must be handled with care. (By the time they get to the second one, they have a better idea of what works and what doesn't, and so they tend not to worry as much – sorry, all of you younger siblings. They still love you very much, but they aren't as prone to worry.)

It's not just mom's that worry; most dad's worry too. Leo Gerstenzang, a Polish immigrant to the United States, was a typical dad. He watched in 1923 as his wife removed their child from the bathtub, laid the child on the changing table, and then reached for a cotton ball. He watched with curiosity as she took a toothpick and placed the cotton ball on the end of it. He didn't say anything, but he watched in horror as she then inserted the cotton ball into their child's ear to remove wax from it.

Horrors filled his mind. What if she slipped and the toothpick poked something vital in the child's ear? What if the cotton ball got stuck in the ear? What if the cotton ball left fibers in the ear? What if the toothpick broke? He was horrified. Fortunately, nothing bad happened to his child that day. However, from the moment on, he knew that he needed to invent a device similar to what his wife created - similar, but much safer.

It took several months of research to design the product and the machine to create the product. However, he eventually made a birch stick with cotton balls tightly wound at both ends. Today, the product is found in most household bathrooms. Although today's doctors discourage people from using the product to remove wax from one's ears, a lot of people still use them for what they were originally designed. They are also used for a lot of other things as well, including dusting in hard-to-reach crevices, applying make-up, and as a paint brush.

Leo called the product Baby Gays, and sold them out of his store, the Leo Gerstenzang Infant Novelty Company. (In the 1920s, "gay" meant "happy", and the product's name was very popular.) In 1926, he changed the name to Quality Tips Baby Gays, and this was soon changed to the name you know the product by . . . *Q-Tips.*

I enjoy jigsaw puzzles. Sometimes I get on a roll and I can find piece after piece. Other times, I can't find a single piece. Sometimes I spend an hour or two trying to find one piece and then, frustrated, I decide to get a shower for the night. As I shower, I suddenly recall where the missing piece is. Most of us have experienced being frustrated, having tried solution after solution, without success, and then doing something else and suddenly having the solution dawn on us.

Charles Goodyear was experiencing those feelings. He had been trying to create weatherproof rubber. Rubber was often used in pencils as erasers and in other products, but if it got too hot, it would crack and break apart. Charles had been experimenting for a long time, believing that such a weatherproof rubber could be created, but he was having no luck finding it. Experiments cost money, and Charles had already been in jail once for not being able to pay his debts, and it appeared that a second time was coming soon. Charles was desperate to find the solution – but it wouldn't come to him.

In his workshop, Charles had a hot stove which he used to keep himself warm. As he experimented, he accidently dropped some regular rubber mixed with sulfur and it landed on the stove. To his amazement, the rubbed maintained its structure; it did not melt under the intense heat. He also found that it had greater strength and was less likely to lose its shape under stress.

Today we use Charles' accidental invention of year-round rubber not only in pencil erasers, but in rubber stamps, automobile tires, garden hoses, birthday balloons, rubber-heeled shoes, rubber bands, rubber gaskets in engines, and much, much more. We don't call it year-round rubber, though, we call it . . . *vulcanized rubber.*

Conclusion

So, what did you think? Pretty interesting, huh?

It's amazing that the things that we take for granted were not available to many generations past; in fact, almost all the inventions in this book were invented in the past 200 years, and people have been on this planet for thousands of years.

What's even more amazing is that even more things will be invented in the future. I can't tell you what daily life will look like 100 years from now, but I can assure you that it will not look like it looks today.

My guess is that you will invent something. It may be a better way to do something; it might be a poem; it might be a snack. (My grandma invented lots of great recipes; she has never gotten famous, but we always enjoy her cooking at family gatherings.) Some people change the entire world; some people just change the world of those around them. What you do makes a difference for others. When you get right down to it, we are all inventors. Some of our inventions are intentional, and others are an unexpected surprise for both us and those around us.

Inventing is fun. As you go through life trying things, don't dwell on the inventions that did not work, focus on the ones that did. Few people can describe how Thomas Edison messed up over 100 times on the lightbulb; they just know he made the lightbulb. You and I are inventors, and, just like the people in this book, we can inspire those around us.

Happy inventing!

Did you enjoy the book?

If you did, we are ecstatic. If not, please write your complaint to us and we will ensure we fix it.

If you're feeling generous, there is something important that you can help me with – tell other people that you enjoyed the book.

Ask a grown-up to write about it on Amazon. When they do, more people will find out about the book. It also lets Amazon know that we are making kids around the world laugh. Even a few words and ratings would go a long way.

If you have any ideas or jokes that you think are super funny, please let us know. We would love to hear from you. Our email address is -

riddleland@riddlelandforkids.com

Riddleland Bonus

Join our Facebook Group at
Riddleland For Kids to get daily jokes and
riddles.

Bonus Book

https://pixelfy.me/riddlelandbonus

Thank you for buying this book. As a token of our appreciation,
we would like to offer a special bonus—a collection of 50
original jokes, riddles, and funny stories.

Other Fun Books By Riddleland
Riddles Series

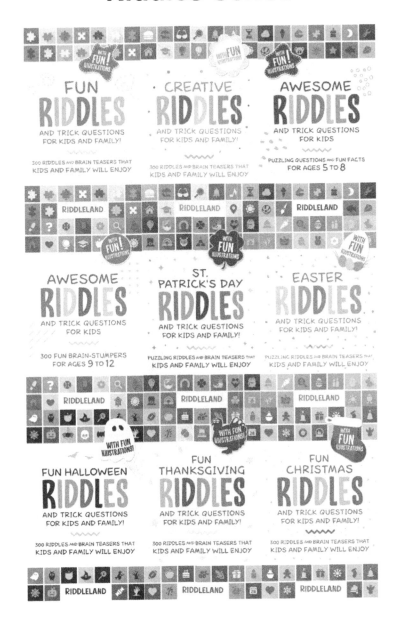

Its Laugh O'Clock Joke Books

It's Laugh O'Clock Would You Rather Books

Get them on Amazon
or our website at **www.riddlelandforkids.com**

REFERENCES

10 inventions that were discovered by accident and changed the world. (2020, October 22).
Retrieved April 02, 2021, from https://dailynewsdig.com/inventions-discovered-accident/

6 outrageous ways to dress up hot dogs (Like mexican Street corn style). (n.d.).
Retrieved April 02, 2021, from https://www.foodnetwork.com/fn-dish/recipes/2016/07/6-outrageous-ways-to-dress-up-hot-dogs-like-mexican-street-corn-style

7 up. (2021, February 26).
Retrieved April 02, 2021, from https://en.wikipedia.org/wiki/7_Up

Accidental discoveries in history: Science / technology. (2013, October 27).
Retrieved April 02, 2021, from https://stephaniehuesler.com/2013/10/19/accidental-discoveries-in-history-science-technology/

The accidental invention of stainless steel. (2018, March 29).
Retrieved April 02, 2021, from https://shapecut.com.au/blog/the-accidental-invention-of-stainless-steel/

The accidental invention of the Coke drink. (2017, December 01).
Retrieved April 02, 2021, from http://www.healthnews.ng/accidental-invention-coke-drink/

Adam Munich. (n.d.).
Retrieved April 02, 2021, from https://adammunich.com/a-brief-history-of-the-x-ray/

Admin. (2019, August 27). Inventor of the pop-up toaster.
Retrieved April 02, 2021, from https://charlesstrite.com/2019/08/27/charles-strite-inventor-of-the-pop-up-toaster/

Aerosol spray. (n.d.).
Retrieved April 02, 2021, from https://www.edinformatics.com/inventions_inventors/aerosol_can.htm

Aldred, J. (2016, August 02). The world's first digital CAMERA, introduced by the man who invented it.
Retrieved April 02, 2021, from https://www.diyphotography.net/worlds-first-digital-camera-introduced-man-invented/

Alexander Graham Bell. (2019, September 09).
Retrieved April 02, 2021, from https://www.biography.com/inventor/alexander-graham-bell

Alexander Graham Bell. (2020, February 20).
Retrieved April 02, 2021, from https://www.bbc.co.uk/bitesize/topics/zxwxvcw/articles/z4vp7nb

Alexandre Godefoy. (n.d.).
Retrieved April 02, 2021, from http://iandijocelyn.weebly.com/

Alfs,L.(2019, January 10). The history of NASHVILLE hot Chicken: How a spurned lover burned millions of mouths.
Retrieved April 02, 2021, from https://www.tennessean.com/story/money/2018/12/20/hot-chicken-nashville-history-princes/2205083002/

Antonie Van Leeuwenhoek. (n.d.).
Retrieved April 02, 2021, from https://www.britannica.com/biography/Antonie-van-Leeuwenhoek

Arthritis. (2019, July 19).
Retrieved April 02, 2021, from https://www.mayoclinic.org/diseases-conditions/arthritis/symptoms-causes/syc-20350772

Arundel Eye Center, A. (2015, July 10). History of THE intraocular Lens (iol): Anne Arundel eye center.
Retrieved April 02, 2021, from https://annearundeleyecenter.com/2015/07/history-of-the-intraocular-lens-iol/

Bada, O. (2018, May 23). Inventions of the world - who invented the toaster?
Retrieved April 02, 2021, from https://www.worldatlas.com/articles/when-was-the-toaster-invented.html

Bakelite. (2021, March 20).
Retrieved April 02, 2021, from https://en.wikipedia.org/wiki/Bakelite

Barrett, A. (2021, February 01). History of cellophane.
Retrieved April 02, 2021, from https://bioplasticsnews.com/2019/07/23/history-of-cellophane/

Behr, F. (2021, January 12). The messed up history Of Lysol.
Retrieved April 02, 2021, from https://www.grunge.com/248173/the-messed-up-history-of-lysol/

Bellis, M. (n.d.). Biography of Antonie van Leeuwenhoek, father of microbiology.
Retrieved April 02, 2021, from https://www.thoughtco.com/anton-van-leeuwenhoek-1991633

Bellis, M. (n.d.). Cellophane invention.
Retrieved April 02, 2021, from http://www.theinventors.org/library/inventors/blcellophane.htm

Bellis, M. (n.d.). Do you know the history of antibiotics?
Retrieved April 02, 2021, from https://www.thoughtco.com/history-of-penicillin-1992304

Bellis, M. (n.d.). Hippocrates discovered Aspirin (he just didn't know it).
Retrieved April 02, 2021, from https://www.thoughtco.com/history-of-aspirin-4072562

Bellis, M. (n.d.). Learn the fascinating history of the x-ray.
Retrieved April 02, 2021, from https://www.thoughtco.com/x-ray-1992692

Bellis, M. (n.d.). Learn the history of Coca-Cola and its Inventor, John Pemberton.
Retrieved April 02, 2021, from https://www.thoughtco.com/history-of-coca-cola-1991477

Bellis, M. (n.d.). Meet the native american who invented potato chips.
Retrieved April 02, 2021, from https://www.thoughtco.com/history-of-potato-chips-1991777

Bellis, M. (n.d.). Play-doh was originally intended to be a wallpaper cleaner.
Retrieved April 02, 2021, from https://www.thoughtco.com/who-invented-play-doh-1992323

Bellis, M. (n.d.). The evolution of aerosol spray cans.
Retrieved April 02, 2021, from https://www.thoughtco.com/history-of-aerosol-spray-cans-1991231

Bellis, M. (n.d.). The history of 7up and Charles Leiper grigg.
Retrieved April 02, 2021, from https://www.thoughtco.com/history-of-7up-charles-leiper-grigg-4075324

Bellis, M. (n.d.). The history of the corkscrew.
Retrieved April 02, 2021, from http://www.theinventors.org/library/weekly/aa122000a.htm

Bellis, M. (n.d.). The history of the Frisbee.
Retrieved April 02, 2021, from https://www.thoughtco.com/history-of-the-frisbee-4072561

Bellis, M. (n.d.). The history of the Goodyear Tire.
Retrieved April 02, 2021, from https://www.thoughtco.com/vulcanized-rubber-1991862

Bellis, M. (n.d.). What year Was Kleenex Tissue first introduced?
Retrieved April 02, 2021, from https://www.thoughtco.com/history-of-kleenex-tissue-1992033

Blitz, M. (2014, September 11). The truth about the origin of the potato chip.
Retrieved April 02, 2021, from http://www.todayifoundout.com/index.php/2014/09/real-story-potato-chip/

Blitz, M. (2018, November 05). How the microwave was invented by accident.
Retrieved April 02, 2021, from https://www.popularmechanics.com/technology/gadgets/a19567/how-the-microwave-was-invented-by-accident/

Brand history I company INFORMATION I Kleenex®. (n.d.).
Retrieved April 2, 2021, from https://www.kleenex.co.uk/kleenex-history

A brief history of snow globes. (2015, December 09).
Retrieved April 02, 2021, from https://www.mentalfloss.com/article/71983/brief-history-snow-globes

Bubble wrap (brand). (2021, February 24).
Retrieved April 02, 2021, from https://en.wikipedia.org/wiki/Bubble_Wrap_(brand)

Butler, S. (2013, August 28). The extra-long history of the hot dog.
Retrieved April 02, 2021, from https://www.history.com/news/break-out-the-buns-the-history-of-the-hot-dog

The California Raisin Industry. (n.d.).
Retrieved April 02, 2021, from https://calraisins.org/about/the-raisin-industry/

Cavanagh, N. (2021, January 13). Why were corn flakes invented?
Retrieved April 02, 2021, from https://www.the-sun.com/news/864463/cornflakes-kelloggs-breakfast-cereal-brothers-history/

Cellophane. (2021, January 27).
Retrieved April 02, 2021, from https://en.wikipedia.org/wiki/Cellophane

Chandler, N. (2020, June 30). What is the history of the remote control?
Retrieved April 02, 2021, from https://science.howstuffworks.com/innovation/repurposed-inventions/history-of-remote-control.htm

Charles Leiper grigg. (2020, August 03).
Retrieved April 02, 2021, from https://en.wikipedia.org/wiki/Charles_Leiper_Grigg

Check out the translation For "NACHO" on SPANISHDICT! (n.d.).
Retrieved April 02, 2021, from https://www.spanishdict.com/translate/nacho

Cheese puffs. (2021, January 09).
Retrieved April 02, 2021, from https://en.wikipedia.org/wiki/Cheese_puffs

Chocolate chip cookie. (2021, March 26).
Retrieved April 02, 2021, from https://en.wikipedia.org/wiki/Chocolate_chip_cookie

Chris. (2017, March 10). Bubble wrap: A short history.
Retrieved April 02, 2021, from https://www.thepackagingcompany.us/knowledge-sharing/bubble-wrap-short-history/

The Coca-Cola Company. (n.d.).
Retrieved April 02, 2021, from https://www.britannica.com/topic/The-Coca-Cola-Company

Cockspur. (n.d.).
Retrieved April 02, 2021, from https://www.dictionary.com/browse/cockspur

Cola history: The Coca-Cola Company. (n.d.).
Retrieved April 02, 2021, from https://www.coca-colacompany.com/company/history

Corkscrew. (2021, March 30).
Retrieved April 02, 2021, from https://en.wikipedia.org/wiki/Corkscrew

Corkscrew. (n.d.).
Retrieved April 02, 2021, from http://www.madehow.com/Volume-6/Corkscrew.html

CorningWare. (2021, January 08).
Retrieved April 02, 2021, from https://en.wikipedia.org/wiki/CorningWare

CuriousHistory. (2017, November 14). History of the hair dryer from 1890 to present day.
Retrieved April 02, 2021, from https://www.curioushistory.com/history-of-the-hair-dryer-from-1890-to-present-day/

Datesman, M. (2017, October 12). Is serendipity the mother of invention?
Retrieved April 02, 2021, from https://vintageamericanways.com/serendipity-mother-invention/

Dennis. (2020, July 13). The history of toaster ovens.
Retrieved April 02, 2021, from https://www.tastemakermag.com/history-toaster-ovens/

Editor. (2020, March 11). The discovery and development of insulin as a medical treatment can be traced back to the 19th century.
Retrieved April 02, 2021, from https://www.diabetes.co.uk/insulin/history-of-insulin.html

Editors of Reminisce. (2017, January 20). Did you know post-it notes were invented by accident?
Retrieved April 02, 2021, from https://www.rd.com/article/post-it-notes-history/

Fabry, M. (2016, April 12). Free cone day history: Who invented ice cream cones?
Retrieved April 02, 2021, from https://time.com/4288576/ice-cream-cone-history/

Facts and history of microwave. (n.d.).
Retrieved April 02, 2021, from http://www.historyofmicrowave.com/

Filippone, P. (n.d.). Raisins are not just an energy-boosting snack food.
Retrieved April 02, 2021, from https://www.thespruceeats.com/raisins-history-and-overview-1807866

Frisbee - history of frisbee. (n.d.).
Retrieved April 02, 2021, from https://softschools.com/inventions/history/frisbee_history/375/

From feeding the US army to going to the moon to making everyday Moments g-r-r-r-eat!. (n.d.).
Retrieved April 02, 2021, from https://www.kelloggs.com/en_US/who-we-are/our-history.html

Fussell, G. (2019, September 30). The origins, history, and design power of neon colors.
Retrieved April 02, 2021, from https://www.shutterstock.com/blog/neon-colors-history-design

Ganninger, D. (2020, May 31). The interesting history of Vaseline (aka Petroleum Jelly).
Retrieved April 02, 2021, from https://medium.com/knowledge-stew/the-interesting-history-of-vaseline-aka-petroleum-jelly-4869e5a6d6e

Garraffo, N. (2016, September 27). The history of bubble wrap.
Retrieved April 02, 2021, from https://abrichards.com/blog/the-history-of-bubble-wrap/

Graham cracker. (2021, March 22).
Retrieved April 02, 2021, from https://en.wikipedia.org/wiki/Graham_cracker

Greenwald, M. (2019, May 23). 30 life-changing inventions that were totally accidental.
Retrieved April 02, 2021, from https://bestlifeonline.com/accidental-inventions/

Gunnarsson, E. (2020, January 31). The history of the computer mouse - how it revolutionized our everyday lives.
Retrieved April 02, 2021, from https://www.soluno.com/computermouse-history/

Hair dryers through the Times TIMELINE. (1890, April 15).
Retrieved April 02, 2021, from https://media.timetoast.com/timelines/hair-dryers-through-the-times

Harry Brearley. (2021, February 12).
Retrieved April 02, 2021, from https://en.wikipedia.org/wiki/Harry_Brearley

Harry Brearley. (n.d.).
Retrieved April 02, 2021, from https://wiki.kidzsearch.com/wiki/Harry_Brearley

Hart, K. (2018, December 18). How the snow globe was accidentally created.
Retrieved April 02, 2021, from https://www.artsy.net/article/artsy-editorial-history-snow-globe

Hiskey, D. (2012, December 03). Post-it notes were invented by accident.
Retrieved April 02, 2021, from http://www.todayifoundout.com/index.php/2011/11/post-it-notes-were-invented-by-accident/

Hiskey, D. (2012, December 03). Silly putty was invented by accident.
Retrieved April 02, 2021, from http://www.todayifoundout.com/index.php/2011/11/silly-putty-was-invented-by-accident/

History - Historic Figures: Antonie van LEEUWENHOEK (1632 - 1723). (n.d.).
Retrieved April 02, 2021, from http://www.bbc.co.uk/history/historic_figures/van_leeuwenhoek_antonie.shtml

The history and science Behind Teflon. (2016, January 19).
Retrieved April 02, 2021, from https://www.product-release.com/product-release-news/history-science-behind-teflon/

The history of a wonderful thing we Call Insulin. (n.d.).
Retrieved April 02, 2021, from https://www.diabetes.org/blog/history-wonderful-thing-we-call-insulin

History of aerosols. (n.d.).
Retrieved April 02, 2021, from https://aeda.org/en/aerosol/history-of-aerosols/

History of aspirin. (n.d.).
Retrieved April 02, 2021, from https://aspirinfo.weebly.com/history-of-aspirin.html

History of basketball. (2021, February 24).
Retrieved April 02, 2021, from https://en.wikipedia.org/wiki/History_of_basketball

History of cheese puffs - how cheese curl is made. (n.d.).
Retrieved April 02, 2021, from http://www.historyofcheese.com/cheese-making/how-are-cheese-curls-made/

History of cheese. (2020, June 19).
Retrieved April 02, 2021, from https://nationalhistoriccheesemakingcenter.org/history-of-cheese/

History of cheese. (2021, March 18).
Retrieved April 02, 2021, from https://en.wikipedia.org/wiki/History_of_cheese

The history of chocolate chip cookies. (n.d.).
Retrieved April 02, 2021, from http://www.kitchenproject.com/history/ChocolateChipCookie/

History of listerine®. (n.d.).
Retrieved April 02, 2021, from https://www.listerine.com/about

History of penicillin. (2021, March 16).
Retrieved April 02, 2021, from https://en.wikipedia.org/wiki/History_of_penicillin

The history of Q-tips - and their original name (which would never ever work today). (2020, January 30).
Retrieved April 02, 2021, from https://clickamericana.com/topics/health-medicine/the-history-of-q-tips-and-their-original-name-which-would-never-ever-work-today

The history of Teflon™ Fluoropolymers. (n.d.).
Retrieved April 02, 2021, from https://www.teflon.com/en/news-events/history

The history of Texting, what you should Know: Signal VINE BLOG. (2018, October 19).
Retrieved April 02, 2021, from https://www.signalvine.com/mobile/the-history-of-texting

The history of the ice cream cone. (2020, January 25).
Retrieved April 02, 2021, from https://www.idfa.org/news-views/media-kits/ice-cream/the-history-of-the-ice-cream-cone

The history of the Microplane. (n.d.).
Retrieved April 02, 2021, from http://kitchenproject.com/history/Microplane/

History of the vulcanization of rubber. (2019, August 03).
Retrieved April 02, 2021, from https://www.globaloring.com/blog/history-of-the-vulcanization-of-rubber/

History.com Editors. (2010, July 30). The invention of the internet.
Retrieved April 02, 2021, from https://www.history.com/topics/inventions/invention-of-the-internet

History.com Staff. (2014, June 08). Who invented basketball?
Retrieved April 02, 2021, from https://www.history.com/news/who-invented-basketball

Horace Wells. (2021, March 30).
Retrieved April 02, 2021, from https://en.wikipedia.org/wiki/Horace_Wells

Hot dog bun. (2021, April 01).
Retrieved April 02, 2021, from https://en.wikipedia.org/wiki/Hot_dog_bun

Hot dog HISTORY: NHDSC. (n.d.).
Retrieved April 02, 2021, from http://www.hot-dog.org/culture/hot-dog-history

How the Microplane moved from the Workshed to the Worktop. (2017, May 19).
Retrieved April 02, 2021, from https://www.independent.co.uk/life-style/food-and-drink/microplane-grater-workshed-worktop-woodwork-tool-a7743361.html

Humphry Davy. (2021, March 28).
Retrieved April 02, 2021, from https://en.wikipedia.org/wiki/Humphry_Davy

Ignacio Anaya. (2021, April 02).
Retrieved April 02, 2021, from https://en.wikipedia.org/wiki/Ignacio_Anaya

Inkjet printing. (2021, March 27).
Retrieved April 02, 2021, from https://en.wikipedia.org/wiki/Inkjet_printing

The innovation school. (2021, March 30).
Retrieved April 02, 2021, from https://www.osa.org/en-us/history/biographies/bios/ichiro_endo/

Insulin (medication). (2021, February 21).
Retrieved April 02, 2021, from https://en.wikipedia.org/wiki/Insulin_(medication)

Intraocular lens. (2021, March 31).
Retrieved April 02, 2021, from https://en.wikipedia.org/wiki/Intraocular_lens

James Naismith. (2021, March 26).
Retrieved April 02, 2021, from https://www.biography.com/scholar/james-a-naismith

Keats, J. (2019, January 02). This immortal coil: How the slinky was born.
Retrieved April 02, 2021, from https://www.wired.com/story/benchmark-slinky-history/

Kids Discover. (2016, August 08). Weird science: The accidental invention of silly putty.
Retrieved April 02, 2021, from http://kidsdiscover.com/quick-reads/weird-science-the-accidental-invention-of-silly-putty/

Kollar, L. (2017, January 31). A brief history of Hot Chicken, Nashville's Spicy Specialty.
Retrieved April 02, 2021, from https://theculturetrip.com/north-america/usa/tennessee/articles/a-brief-history-of-hot-chicken-nashvilles-spicy-specialty/

Labs, A. (n.d.). Evolution of text messaging and rcs.
Retrieved April 02, 2021, from https://www.snapdesk.app/text-messaging-history-timeline-evolution-rcs/

Lall, T. (2020, April 17). 15 things you can Use Listerine for apart from cleaning your mouth.
Retrieved April 02, 2021, from https://www.scoopwhoop.com/Listerine-uses/

Lamoureux, A. (2020, April 27). Lysol was once used as birth control – and poisoned a lot of women.
Retrieved April 02, 2021, from https://allthatsinteresting.com/lysol-birth-control

Latest medical NEWS, clinical Trials, guidelines - today on Medscape. (n.d.).
Retrieved April 02, 2021, from https://www.medscape.com/slideshow/accidental-discoveries-6008976

Leo Baekeland and invention of Bakelite. (n.d.).
Retrieved April 02, 2021, from http://www.historyofplastic.com/plastic-inventor/leo-baekeland/

Leo Baekeland. (2021, March 29).
Retrieved April 02, 2021, from https://en.wikipedia.org/wiki/Leo_Baekeland

Levitt, A. (2019, December 03). The inventor of the MICROPLANE hopes someone still uses it for woodworking.
Retrieved April 02, 2021, from https://thetakeout.com/microplane-invention-grace-manufacturing- 1840173728

Listerine. (2021, March 27).
Retrieved April 02, 2021, from https://en.wikipedia.org/wiki/Listerine

LLC, A. (n.d.). The history of cat litter.
Retrieved April 02, 2021, from https://www.cathealth.com/cat-care/accessories/2508-the-history-of-cat-litter

Lysol. (2021, March 27).
Retrieved April 02, 2021, from https://en.wikipedia.org/wiki/Lysol

Markel, H., Dr. (2013, September 27). The real story behind penicillin.
Retrieved April 02, 2021, from https://www.pbs.org/newshour/health/the-real-story-behind-the-worlds-first-antibiotic

McDonald's. (2017, July 07). The making of a Happy meal - MCDONALD'S india: Mcdonald's blog.
Retrieved April 02, 2021, from https://mcdonaldsblog.in/2015/10/the-making-of-a-happy-meal/

Mertes, A. (2021, March 02). Who invented the mouse pad & why?
Retrieved April 02, 2021, from https://www.qualitylogoproducts.com/blog/who-invented-the-mouse-pad/

Moncel, B. (n.d.). How has cheese changed through history?
Retrieved April 02, 2021, from https://www.thespruceeats.com/the-history-of-cheese-1328765

Moss, R. (2020, May 13). The complete history of ice cream cones.
Retrieved April 02, 2021, from https://www.seriouseats.com/2019/06/ice-cream-cone-history.html

Mousepad. (2021, February 26).
Retrieved April 02, 2021, from https://en.wikipedia.org/wiki/Mousepad

Mudgal, S. (2019, August 21). The story behind the origin of corn flakes is so bizarre you'll find it hard to digest.
Retrieved April 02, 2021, from https://www.scoopwhoop.com/news/origins-story-of-kelloggs-corn-flakes/

Nachos. (2021, March 29).
Retrieved April 02, 2021, from https://en.wikipedia.org/wiki/Nachos

Nguyen, T. (n.d.). Here's how World War II led to duct tape.
Retrieved April 02, 2021, from https://www.thoughtco.com/history-of-duct-tape-4040012

Our values. (n.d.).
Retrieved April 02, 2021, from https://www.kelloggcompany.com/en_US/about-kellogg-company.html

Penicillin discovered by Sir Alexander Fleming. (2010, February 09).
Retrieved April 02, 2021, from https://www.history.com/this-day-in-history/penicillin-discovered

Person. (2020, February 04). History of raisin " iran dried fruit.
Retrieved April 02, 2021, from https://www.irandriedfruit.com/raisin-history/

Pies, F. (n.d.). Our story.
Retrieved April 02, 2021, from https://www.frisbiepie.com/our_story/

Play-doh. (2021, February 04).
Retrieved April 02, 2021, from https://en.wikipedia.org/wiki/Play-Doh

Popsicle fun Facts: Mobile cuisine. (2020, August 26).
Retrieved April 02, 2021, from https://mobile-cuisine.com/did-you-know/popsicle-fun-facts/

The popsicle® Story. (n.d.).
Retrieved April 02, 2021, from https://www.popsicle.com/our-story/

Post-it notes - invented by accident! (2014, December 12).
Retrieved April 02, 2021, from https://medium.com/the-history-of-office-supplies-and-equipment/post-it-notes-invented-by-accident-1f3427da7d59

Potato chip. (2021, March 23).
Retrieved April 02, 2021, from https://en.wikipedia.org/wiki/Potato_chip

Q-tips - history of q-tips. (n.d.).
Retrieved April 02, 2021, from https://www.softschools.com/inventions/history/q_tips_history/283/

Qazi, A. (2020, February 29). Brief timeline of a toaster oven - a history lesson.
Retrieved April 02, 2021, from https://kitchengearoid.com/toaster-ovens/brief-timeline-of-a-toaster-oven/

Reindl, A. (2019, September 18). The mcdonalds happy meal was invented by a latina and here's how it got started.
Retrieved April 02, 2021, from https://wearemitu.com/entertainment/did-you-know-the-first-happy-meal-was-invented-by-a-latina/

Roberts, S. (2020, December 29). What is NASHVILLE Hot Chicken?
Retrieved April 02, 2021, from http://scottroberts.org/what-is-nashville-hot-chicken/

Sarah. (2017, March 16). The history of glow sticks.
Retrieved April 02, 2021, from https://www.glowtopia.co.uk/news/history-of-glowsticks/

Scientist discovers x-rays. (2009, November 24).
Retrieved April 02, 2021, from https://www.history.com/this-day-in-history/german-scientist-discovers-x-rays

Sharkey, B. (2018, September 08). This map shows you what people CALL soda pop in every part of country.
Retrieved April 02, 2021, from https://www.simplemost.com/here-is-what-people-call-soda-pop-in-every-part-of-country/

Sharp, M. (2015, June 17). History of chocolate chip cookies.
Retrieved April 02, 2021, from https://facts-about-chocolate.com/history-of-chocolate-chip-cookies/

Silentstrike. (2016, January 31). Accidental inventions – smart dust.
Retrieved April 02, 2021, from https://strikecyberscoop.wordpress.com/2016/01/31/accidental-inventions-smart-dust/

Simmons, A. (2021, March 23). 10 accidental discoveries that changed the world.
Retrieved April 02, 2021, from https://www.rd.com/list/10-accidental-discoveries-put-to-good-use/

Skipworth, H. (2019, January 25). Timeline: The history of digital cameras.
Retrieved April 02, 2021, from https://www.digitalspy.com/tech/cameras/a591251/world-photography-day-2014-the-history-of-digital-cameras/

Slinky. (2021, March 26).
Retrieved April 02, 2021, from https://en.wikipedia.org/wiki/Slinky

Slinky. (n.d.).
Retrieved April 02, 2021, from https://www.toyhalloffame.org/toys/slinky

Smartdust. (2021, March 22).
Retrieved April 02, 2021, from https://en.wikipedia.org/wiki/Smartdust

Snow globe. (2021, March 26).
Retrieved April 02, 2021, from https://en.wikipedia.org/wiki/Snow_globe

The surprising origins of the tv remote. (n.d.).
Retrieved April 02, 2021, from https://www.bbc.com/future/article/20180830-the-history-of-the-television-remote-control

Tidy cats legacy. (n.d.).
Retrieved April 02, 2021, from https://www.purina.com/tidy-cats/cat-litter-info

The toaster oven. (n.d.).
Retrieved April 02, 2021, from https://ashawbcd.weebly.com/the-toaster-oven.html

Trenholm, R. (n.d.). Photos: The history of the digital camera.
Retrieved April 02, 2021, from https://www.cnet.com/news/photos-the-history-of-the-digital-camera/

Vaseline. (2021, March 27).
Retrieved April 02, 2021, from https://en.wikipedia.org/wiki/Vaseline

Vulcanization. (n.d.).
Retrieved April 02, 2021, from https://www.britannica.com/technology/vulcanization

Wang, K. (2020, August 18). 18 things you didn't know about the history of fast food.
Retrieved April 02, 2021, from https://www.buzzfeed.com/kimberlywang/the-history-of-fast-food

Weird science: The accidental invention of silly putty. (2020, January 17).
Retrieved April 02, 2021, from https://www.wikye.com/weird-science-the-accidental-invention-of-silly-putty/

White, D. (2020, November 27). Why were Graham Crackers invented?
Retrieved April 02, 2021, from https://www.thesun.co.uk/news/13315887/why-graham-crackers-invented/

White, R. (2019, January 10). The history of pop-up toasters.
Retrieved April 02, 2021, from https://oureverydaylife.com/the-history-of-pop-up-toasters-12210962.html

Who invented playdough? (n.d.).
Retrieved April 02, 2021, from https://www.wonderopolis.org/wonder/who-invented-play-dough

Who invented the internet? (2018, November 13).
Retrieved April 02, 2021, from https://www.computerhope.com/issues/ch001016.htm

Who invented the internet? (n.d.).
Retrieved April 02, 2021, from https://www.britannica.com/story/who-invented-the-internet

Who invented the microwave? (n.d.).
Retrieved April 02, 2021, from https://www.reference.com/history/invented-microwave-16a9930c6d5f0b36

Who we are. (n.d.).
Retrieved April 02, 2021, from https://www.vaseline.com/arabia/en/who-we-are.html

Why we say hello when answering the phone and not...ahoy!? (2018, October 08).
Retrieved April 02, 2021, from https://apolloansweringservice.com/why-we-say-hello-when-answering-the-phone/

Wilde, L. (2013, September 04). The history of cat litter and litter boxes.
Retrieved April 02, 2021, from https://catwisdom101.com/history-cat-litter-litter-boxes/

William Murdoch. (2021, March 04).
Retrieved April 02, 2021, from https://en.wikipedia.org/wiki/William_Murdoch

William S. Hadaway (1866-1953) - find a grave... (n.d.).
Retrieved April 02, 2021, from https://www.findagrave.com/memorial/13630222/william-s.-hadaway

Wilson, J. (2021, March 01). 10 effective brainstorming techniques for teams.
Retrieved April 02, 2021, from https://www.wework.com/ideas/worklife/effective-brainstorming-techniques

Wohleber, C. (n.d.). Duct tape.
Retrieved April 02, 2021, from https://www.inventionandtech.com/content/duct-tape-0

Wong, E. (2013, June 19). Inventions that were accidents.
Retrieved April 02, 2021, from https://www.forbes.com/2010/12/23/ten-accidental-inventions-leadership-cmo-network-common.html

WorldTopUpdates. (2017, November 10). Accidental funny inventions that brought a change to the world.
Retrieved April 02, 2021, from https://www.worldtopupdates.com/funny-inventions-that-changed-the-world/

The Zen Cart® Team and others. (n.d.). Classic kitchens and MORE, AUTHENTIC RETRO Kitchenware.
Retrieved April 02, 2021, from http://www.classickitchensandmore.com

Made in the USA
Middletown, DE
04 June 2022

66664864R00084